# APL: Developing more flexible colleges

Further education: the assessment and accreditation
of prior learning series
Edited by Norman Evans and Michèle Bailleux, both
of the Learning from Experience Trust

In the same series

**APL: Equal opportunities for all**
*Cecilia McKelvey and Helen Peters*

**Introducing APEL**
*Maggie Challis*

# APL: Developing more flexible colleges

## Michael Field

London and New York

First published 1993
by Routledge
11 New Fetter Lane, London EC4P 4EE

Transferred to Digital Printing 2004

Simultaneously published in the USA and Canada
by Routledge Inc.
29 West 35th Street, New York, NY 10001

Typeset in Palatino by LaserScript, Mitcham, Surrey

*British Library Cataloguing in Publication Data*
A catalogue record for this book is available from the British Library

ISBN 0–415–09015–6

*Library of Congress Cataloging in Publication Data*
Field, Michael, 1940–
  APL: developing more flexible colleges/Michael Field.
  p. cm. – (Further education)
  Includes index.
  ISBN 0–415–09015–6
  1. Experiential learning – Great Britain. 2. Universities and
  colleges – Great Britain – Administration. 3. College credits –
  Great Britain. I. Title. II. Series: Further education
  (London, England)
  LB2353.67.F54   1993
  370.15'23 – dc20                                    93-7216
                                                         CIP

ISBN 0–415–09015–6

This book is dedicated to four people, each of whom had a significant impact on my life and personal development.

The late Reg Pepper, friend, task master and sometime employer who signposted the earlier paths of my life.

Sid Lowe, teacher and friend who showed me how to succeed professionally.

Alan Body, colleague and friend who taught me that educational management was about people and not numbers.

The late Bill Pasquerella, friend and advisor who was always there when I needed him, and is now sadly missed.

Special thanks also to Graeme Hill, for providing all the illustrations contained in the text.

# Contents

# Figures and tables

# Series Editors' foreword

This book is an attempt to show what a college needs to think about before introducing schemes for the assessment and accreditation of prior and experiential learning. It goes on to show what a college needs to set about doing, if it is serious about its intentions with prior and experiential learning.

The book is organised so that at the beginning the principles and practice of the assessment of prior and experiential learning are laid out, together with the reasons why its introduction is a critical factor for colleges as they face the new requirements being laid upon them.

The first chapter provides the obligato for the management tunes which run through the chapters which follow; a kind of background theme song which runs quietly without being explicitly articulated. It is the essential reference point. As Mike Field says on his very first page, '. . . the provision by a college of the accreditation of prior learning, along with all the support services needed to ensure its success, can be used as the "acid test" of whether a college is truly open and accessible to a wide variety of learners'.

*APL: developing more flexible colleges* has several purposes. It is a volume by an author rooted in the experience he draws on, intended to be of some value to other senior figures in further education who are facing the problems that he has tried to deal with. As such it could be a useful tool for those who have direct responsibility for implementing the changes which they face. But it is also intended for those tutors who plan and run courses to help academic and administrative staff come to terms with the new world which they are entering. And of course there are those who find general interest in reading about change in one sector because they can find clues about what is going on in their own.

At the same time it is a book which seeks to set the stage for a number of books which will follow, each concentrating on particular aspects of some applications of the assessment and accreditation of prior and experiential learning in further education.

APL cannot be bolt-on additions to what a college has done traditionally. That way lies disaster. That is the message of this book. And hence its importance as the first one in this series.

Norman Evans, Director, Learning from Experience Trust
Michèle Bailleux, Deputy Director, Learning from Experience Trust

# Foreword to the series

In Britain, the assessment and accreditation of prior learning (APL) began with the assessment of prior experiential learning (APEL). When discussion first began about APEL and further education, accreditation of anything other than examined outcomes was hardly on the map. Partly this was because APEL was seen as an additional way of widening access. But also it was because self-assessment stood out as one of the richest dividends for individuals from APEL. Accreditation might follow, but that was a separate issue. Over time, and that means from the early 1980s, the term APL has come to refer to all previously acquired learning, which necessarily includes experiential learning. So whereas APEL refers specifically to uncertificated learning, APL refers to that as well as to previous learning that has been formally certificated through some recognised examining body. Both are vital. So often the one can lead to the other and both can serve as approach routes to additional formal learning. Throughout the books in this series, this distinction needs to be borne in mind. Perhaps the easiest way is to think of APEL as a subset of APL. And now, of course, accreditation is a lively issue for both.

Discussions about introducing the assessment of prior experiential learning to formal education in Britain began with higher education in the early 1980s.. About two years later, further education entered the arena in two ways. Jack Mansell, then Chief Officer of the Further Education Unit, commissioned a project which resulted in the publication in 1984 of *Curriculum Opportunity: a map of experiential learning in entry requirements to higher and further education award-bearing courses.* Alun Davies, then the Chief Inspector for Higher and Further Education in the Inner London Education Authority, recognised the potential of

APEL for further education as an influence on curriculum reform, staff development and for assisting colleges to prepare for a future that was going to be different from the past and present. So he gave a brief to a success of enthusiastic and energetic staff in the Curriculum Development Unit to promote APEL activities in colleges wherever they could.

As some staff moved on to other posts inside and outside London, APEL activities spread so that by the time the National Council for Vocational Qualifications was established in 1986, there were staff in a number of further education colleges who had gone some way towards developing schemes for APEL, some of them promoted by the FEU, some of them connected with REPLAN projects for the unemployed. The Unit for the Development of Adult and Continuing Education took a hand through its programme of work on Access. And as Open College Federations and Networks worked at ways of awarding official recognition to non-institutional, off-campus learning, so they added yet another strand to APEL activities. As the benefits of progression and credit accumulation began to be more widely appreciated, both APL and APEL became an increasingly important dimension to Access, while NCVQ gave a strong lead in that direction through its own version of Prior Learning Achievements.

Now colleges face a different and uncertain future. It seems that to remain effective as incorporated institutions, they have to find ways of supplementing their funding from the FEFC, while pursuing policies designed to increase and widen participation. That means evolving imaginative forms of collaboration with industry and commerce. It means finding viable ways of handling Vocational Qualifications. And it all poses difficult organisational issues for a college that sets out to meet that range of requirements. So APL and APEL have become deadly serious considerations, so much so that it would be hard to walk into any college without finding people who were talking about both. And often at the heart of those discussions there is the tension between using both APL and APEL for personal development and as a component of liberal education and seeing them as part of the provision for Vocational Qualifications.

In the real world of day-to-day activity in colleges, however, there is more talk than action. This is not surprising. Incorporating APL as mainstream activity rather then seeing it as something rather fancy at the margins, touches issues from the top to the bottom of any institution. Overall management, academic organisation, the curriculum, modes of learning, teaching styles and delivery, admissions, student guidance and support systems, assessment procedures, relations with awarding bodies and NCVQ and, more recently, with higher education through franchising and associated status, all come into the reckoning. And since, as the books in this series imply, flexibility needs to be the hallmark of successful colleges in the future, and the effective introduction of APL requires flexibility, the message is clear. Colleges need APL to be flexible, effectively. APL requires flexibility to be successful within an institution.

This series of books on Further Education: the Assessment and Accreditation of Prior Learning, is a contribution towards encouraging colleges to incorporate APL schemes as mainstream provision. Moreover, we hope that because each of these books is written by men and women who know what they are talking about from their direct professional experience in the theory and practice of APL and APEL, whatever the particular focus of their writing, they will be of practical help to colleges and college staff wishing to develop schemes of their own.

Norman Evans, Director, Learning from Experience Trust
Michèle Bailleux, Deputy Director, Learning from Experience Trust
London, 1992

# Introduction

This book examines a number of issues which colleges will have
to face as they make moves to increase their flexibility and
responsiveness and meet new client needs. The first chapter con-
centrates on the introduction of the accreditation of prior learning
and includes a framework for change. The next chapter begins
with a description of the historical forces which shaped today's
colleges, followed by an outline of the external pressures
currently being placed on them to reshape their services to meet
new demands.

Other early chapters explore the range of responses being
made by colleges to increase access, along with the range of
opportunities which they provide to enable individuals to gain
recognition and accreditation for their learning. The responses
reviewed include ways in which colleges are reshaping their
traditional teaching and learning programmes coupled with new
ways of achieving accreditation through the recognition of work-
based learning plus new and assessment services. All these
responses when linked together will create the forces which will
shape tomorrow's colleges.

The middle chapters of the book outline the need for
tomorrow's colleges to develop their own distinct mission, widen
participation, effectively attract potential students and support
them in ways which enable them to succeed.

Later chapters of the book review some of the organisational
factors affecting flexibility. The issues surrounding the management of change, frameworks for bringing about change and
managing resistance to it are examined in some detail.

# Chapter 1

# The alternative focus of accreditation of prior learning

It is widely acknowledged that the introduction of the Further and Higher Education Act has brought post-sixteen education to the brink of a new era. The watchwords of this era will be flexibility of response, open access, equality of opportunity and valuing and accrediting alternative ways of learning, linked together within the concept of providing life-long learning opportunities. These developments are the focus of this book which takes as its theme the accreditation of prior learning, because the availability of accreditation of alternative ways of learning is one of the main measures against which the true flexibility and openness of colleges can be assessed. Indeed, it can be argued that such accreditation, along with the support services needed to ensure its success, can be used as the acid test of whether a college is truly open and accessible to a wide variety of learners.

It provides this acid-test because it cuts across most, if not all, of the systems currently used to manage colleges. Consequently, it does not fit neatly into the organisational arrangements used by colleges to structure the use of staff time and accommodate their current main business of providing structured programmes for teaching and learning. It therefore gives a glimpse into the problems of providing the flexibility which will be the essential requirement of colleges in the future. It demands a new approach which focuses on the specific needs of individuals rather than the established one of concentrating on the aggregated needs of groups of learners.

Accreditation of prior learning (APL) is based on the acceptance and recognition that learning can and does take place in a wide variety of traditional and non-traditional situations. It treats them all as being of equal value to the learning which takes place in more traditional teaching and learning situations.

## INTRODUCING ACCREDITATION

As already pointed out (see p. 1), the introduction of the accreditation of prior learning into a college cuts across most of the existing systems of resource allocation and control, most of which were designed to cater for a more 'steady state', based on the notion that students will be in fairly stable groupings for most of their time at college. These kinds of systems cannot accommodate the amount of flexibility required to handle students who do not attend college on a regular basis. There are many problems to be faced in order to introduce large, open, flexible learning centres and assessment on demand. The required changes will include:

- new ways of information giving
- recording information enquiries for follow-up purposes
- continuous enrolment
- enrolment for roll on/roll off programmes
- assessment on demand
- extended counselling and guidance
- accreditation of prior learning
- mix and match modulisation
- enrolment in flexible learning centres
- students following individual learning contracts
- the assessment of work-based learning
- involvement in learning networks
- flexible resourcing
- flexible fee charging
- alternative modes of attendance and non-attendance.

The philosophy underlying the structure of this book is that successful colleges will in some measure share the following characteristics:

- they will be customer focused
- they will have a clear sense of mission
- they will have built-in responsiveness to change
- they will operate as learning organisations
- they will be efficient and active resource managers
- they will focus on creating space for freedom of action.

## Customer focus

Successful colleges set out to know their customers well and make the satisfying of customer needs the focus of all their actions. They do this by developing and maintaining close links with direct and indirect customers.

- Direct customers include:

  - potential students
  - enrolled students
  - companies/firms which will employ students at the end of their studies
  - other educational institutions which receive students into their programmes

- Indirect customers include:

  - sponsors: parents, employers training agencies, etc.
  - consultative committees representing the users or sponsors of students
  - other organisations such as chambers of commerce, professional and community based organisations

- Customer support is extended through:

  - personal support – information giving, counselling and tutoring
  - monitoring and reporting progress
  - after sales service when client has left the college.

## A sense of mission

Successful colleges have a clear sense of mission which:

- describes the kind of institution they are striving to become
- sets out their values ethos, style and organisation's climate
- develops ownership to the point where it is shared and supported by staff and governors
- is apparent in the actions and behaviour of all staff, and translated into action by:

  - clarity about the values of the college and how they should influence behaviour
  - prioritising the aims into measurable objectives

♦ setting them out in a statement of corporate strategy in the form of a three year rolling plan supported by annual operating statements
♦ developing organisational and administrative structures which provide for successful achievement of the plan.
♦ closely monitoring and controlling progress towards the objectives set out in the plan.

### Responsiveness to change

Successful colleges will be responsive to changing client needs and introduce any required changes quickly. Their attention will therefore be focused on ensuring that:

• they develop and maintain a comprehensive programme of educational/training opportunities linked to new ways of enabling individuals to succeed by recognising that learning takes place in a variety of situations
• they reflect the needs and aspirations of the community they serve and are perceptive of and responsive to changes in these needs
• they have the facility to innovate and lead in the development of new types of provision
• they maintain a high level of quality and relevance within their programmes

### Learning organisations

Successful colleges will see themselves as 'learning organisations' which learn from doing and focus on the development of their staff and systems in line with changing needs. Learning from doing means:

• accepting risk taking in decisions and being prepared to get things wrong when dealing with uncertainty and change
• learning through review and contemplation how things can be done better next time
• This means ensuring that there are:

♦ sound and effective systems of staff management and industrial relations
♦ clear and active support policies for staff development and training, covering both the teaching and teaching support staff.

## Resource management

Successful colleges will control their resources tightly and use them creatively in funding their objectives. This will be done by:

- optimising if not maximising the use of all resources available at all times
- funding the strategic operating plans
- getting decision-making and accountability as close as possible to the points where action is initiated
- having tight monitoring and control systems which measure progress towards objectives and the cost effectiveness of all activities.

## Freedom of action

Successful colleges are always looking for ways in which they can create time and space for freedom of action to respond to change. They achieve this by searching for administrative systems which:

- limit bureaucracy and keep paperwork to a minimum
- are supportive and not restrictive of the college's ability to satisfy student needs
- underpin the curriculum
- provide open systems of communication which link together all other management systems and keep staff informed.

These then are the characteristics which will underpin the success or otherwise of tomorrow's colleges. They support the pressures to increase flexibility of response, equality of opportunity and accrediting alternative ways of learning. These pressures for change are the focus of the chapters which follow. All these needs will have to be met by tomorrow's colleges and most of them result from the introduction of accreditation of prior learning, which is why it is such a good acid test for the future.

As already discussed (see p. 1), the introduction of accreditation represents a high profile change which impacts on most of a college's established services. Such a change requires careful planning and implementation strategies if it is to succeed. The following framework illustrates the stages and tasks involved in planning and satisfactorily bringing about the changes required for the introduction of the accreditation of prior learning:

| *Activity/preparation* | *Problem to overcome* |
|---|---|
| *Pre-planning* | |
| • Define the objectives required to be met and the criteria for assessing their progress | • Identification of potential population for accreditation<br>• Identification of areas of assessment to be offered<br>• Resources necessary to satisfy the market to be set out |
| • Identify staff/resources requirements | • Identification of staff required for<br>  – information giving<br>  – advisory interviews<br>  – counselling<br>  – assessment<br>• Development of assessment network<br>• Necessary training to be arranged and provided<br>• Identification of space/rooms needed<br>• Identification of costs and income projection<br>• Allocation of funding |
| • Promotion/ communications | • Promotional materials to be devised and printed<br>• Concept of accreditation to be internally promoted and its benefits communicated to all staff |
| *Planning and implementation* | |
| • Identify options for the methods of providing accreditation | • Generation of ideas for planning and implementation by consultation with relevant colleagues and external consultants |

- Define staff strategies to be used to support the introduction of accreditation
  - awareness raising activities
  - needs identification
  - allocating staff resources
  - information giving
  - fee setting
  - enrolment
  - registration
  - accounting for staff time
  - obtaining value for the work done
  - payment of counsellors and assessors

*Monitoring and controlling*
- Define how objectives will be measured and processes be controlled

- Development of approaches which attempt to balance cost and effectiveness with quality of service
- Focus needed on what is technically possible with the staff/resources available
- Maximisation of internal expertise
  - staff with cross-college responsibilities
  - other interest groups
  - existing networks between any of the above
  - relevant groups working on flexibility
- Identification of areas where external expertise may be needed
- Identification of the support team for introducing and managing the accreditation processes

- Identification of key responsibilities

- Clarification of targets and time frames
- Clarification with all the staff involved
  - their individual and collective responsibilities
  - their communication procedures
  - their formal reporting, monitoring and evaluation procedures

### Further development

- Decide what arrangements have to be made to obtain feedback on potential improvements

- Evaluation of the support procedures necessary for accreditation
- Clarification of mecchanisms for
  - providing feedback on progress and areas for future improvement
  - deciding how priority issues are to be raised and processed
  - deciding how suggested improvements are to be fed into the next planning cycle
- Which curriculum areas are next to be added to the list of accreditation options?

*Source*: Amended from the Assessment of Prior Learning and Learner Services by kind permission of the FEU. Research by Corinne Henebery.

# Chapter 2

# The shaping of today's colleges

Today's colleges are the result of the way in which further education has developed since its beginnings. During this development colleges were required to offer a menu of courses suitable to the needs of the community, industry or commerce they served. This menu usually displayed the following characteristics:

1 Structure

   (a) structured on a programme of subject-focused courses, built around job-specific skills, general education, or personal development;
   (b) offered as a timetable at pre-determined set times, covering a fixed academic year which ran from September to July;
   (c) mostly teacher centred in terms of style and learning structures, and teacher controlled in terms of programme presentation, pace and direction;

2 Underlying skills

   (a) knowledge of qualification pathways, built around an understanding of entry requirements to courses and examinations;
   (b) ability to arrange course, room and staff timetables to meet the requirements of a tightly set menu of course programmes;
   (c) a match to examination requirements between the presentation skills of teachers and note taking for students;

3 Support systems: the outcome of the above programme characteristics and skill requirements is that the architecture of colleges has resulted in:

(a) buildings dominated by teaching spaces divided into small or large general teaching rooms, dedicated specialist rooms and practical workshops;

(b) buildings are supported by specialist technician services focused on servicing the teaching spaces and providing equipment or audio visual support to teachers rather than learners;

(c) programmes are also provided with reprographics support for teaching materials, and other more general facilities such as library/resource centres and administrative back-up;

4 Management systems: colleges have inherited management control systems which focus on measures of efficiency based on the notion that all teaching takes place in large groups, in single rooms, under the direction of one teacher. Prime examples are measures of efficiency such as student/staff ratios (SSRs), average class sizes (ACS) and average lecture hours (ALH). These measures do not adequately measure the more flexible ways of structuring and accrediting achievement being developed by today's colleges. For example, the system does not know how to measure or credit such work as assessment on demand or accreditation of prior learning (APL).

The inter-related nature of all these characteristics on the shaping of today's colleges can be seen in Figure 2.1.

DEVELOPING PRESSURES

Given the inheritance of today's colleges in their architecture and management systems the real question is to what extent are they in the position of being able to respond to growing pressures to:

• move towards the introduction of life-long learning approaches across all the education/training programmes offered by colleges
• offer opportunities for credit accumulation across different programmes
• structure programmes away from set menus towards modules of learning and assessment
• offer accreditation of prior learning, assisted by adequate guidance and other back-up facilities.

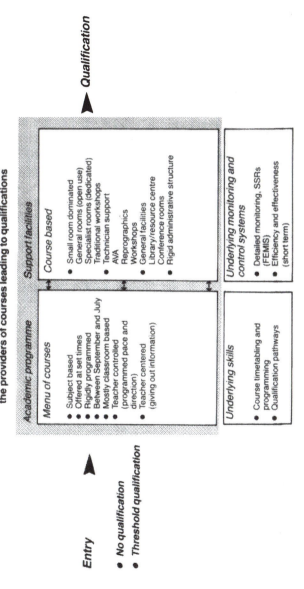

*Figure 2.1* The inter-relationship of characteristics shaping today's colleges

## EXTERNAL PRESSURES FOR CHANGE

Colleges have always responded to change. The approach of this book is based on the assumption that they will continue to be proactive in their response to the two general kinds of change which they will increasingly face:

1 Continuous or predictable changes for which they can plan and prepare, based on past experiences;
2 Unpredictable or discontinuous change which will require new kinds of responses often within a short time period.

In the past, continuous predictable change has been the dominant force, but if colleges are to continue to reflect the needs of society they will increasingly have to respond to discontinuous change. The first major pressure which will shape them will be the changing ratio between predictable and unpredictable change, illustrated in Figure 2.2. Both kinds of change will have to be accommodated within the strategic thinking of colleges. As they move forward, colleges will need to become more skilled at assessing the impact of any change on the services they currently provide in terms of:

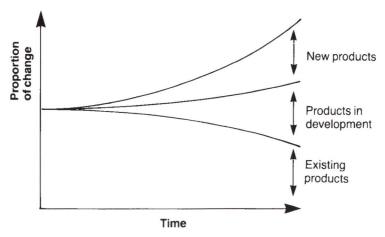

**Growth objectives through innovation**

*Figure 2.2* The changing nature of change

1  Its nature: whether it will have a slight or profound effect on existing programme patterns;
2  Its pace: the speed with which the change will take place and the response time needed from the college;
3  Its direction: what it is affecting, what things will need to change.

These three factors can be further sub-divided into two general areas:

(a) changes affecting the structure and content of programmes and their methods of delivery;
(b) changes affecting the usefulness of the output (students) of college programmes, particularly related to ensuring that programme content is up to date and related to its utility in life generally and employment in particular.

Colleges will therefore need to assess change in terms of its impact on their different client groups, such as:

• those in full-time education as a preparation for higher education or the world of employment
• those in employment
• those out of employment
• those specifically aiming to re-enter employment
• those wishing to undertake personal development.

For all these client groups relevance, responsiveness, flexibility and openness will be key features of the college's response to change.

## Imposed changes in the curriculum

The curriculum frameworks offered by colleges have always been the subject of both continuous and discontinuous changes. In the past these changes have been evolutionary and have taken place at a much slower pace than the pressures for change being experienced by colleges today. Given the pace of change in society generally and in industry and commerce it is unlikely that the pace of change will slacken in the near future. Depending on the needs of their catchment areas and on the market segments they serve, colleges will need to have well thought through strategies for implementing the following changes:

- the introduction of a comprehensive framework of National Vocational Qualifications (NVQs) linked to the achievement of National Education and Training Targets
- the introduction of General National Vocational Qualifications (GNVQs) and their impact on existing provision
- programmes designed to provide equality of esteem between academic and vocational qualifications including the introduction of ordinary and advanced diplomas
- the position of 'A' levels and the promotion of 'AS' qualifications
- publication by law of examination results
- extension of training credits to day-release students in 1996
- extension of achievement-focused funding
- the development of self-validating institutions and their effects on some of the HE provision offered in FE colleges.

## The changing education/training needs of those in employment

There are changes in the education/training needs of those in employment to which colleges will need to respond as they review and reshape their provision. Although many of these changes are well known to college managers the increased numbers of those taking up places at age sixteen has moved the focus. As the number of sixteen-year-old entrants declines, consideration will have to move more towards:

- Demand for a higher skilled workforce: the introduction of new technology, particularly in the rapidly changing fields of information technology, will require higher skill levels from operatives. These skills must be provided either for those entering employment or by the re-skilling of existing workers. Colleges will need to become more flexible in catering for these needs.
- The growth of knowledge workers: the number of such workers is increasing, as evidenced by the increase in the managerial, professional and technical categories of employment. Knowledge workers are often critical to the success of the organisations they work for, so if the organisation wishes to remain competitive it must invest in ways of keeping its knowledge workers up-to-date and effective. Much of this training may be done by the organisation itself. Colleges may see opportunities to support this kind of training by offering the accreditation of work-based learning linked to the training

being provided, along with assessment on demand and other support services. For those organisations too small to provide the necessary up-date training, colleges may wish to develop partnership agreements to provide off-the-job training linked to work-based learning.

- The development of a higher educated/trained workforce: with the increase of students entering and graduating from colleges and universities, the workforce is set to become progressively higher educated. In addition, the setting of national training targets for both foundation and life-long learning should have the effect of raising the general level of competence of the workforce. These developments require new responses from colleges, particularly in establishing partnership schemes with industry along with the accreditation of work-based learning and other assessment and accreditation services.

- The growth of homeworking and self-managing workers: for some time observers have been predicting a steady growth of self-managing workers. There is now ample evidence that such workers have arrived both within organisations in the form of semi-autonomous working groups, or as self-employed, sub-contractors or home-based workers.

  They need a high level of personal skill and the ability to be self-managing problem solvers. They are required to plan their own work based on its inter-relationship and dependence on other activities and workers. With this goes the responsibility to exercise their own quality control, and to meet the requirements of both internal and external customers.

  Because of the pressure on their time, the demands for access to new learning opportunities from self-employed, self-managed workers does not fit easily into the kind of provision offered by most colleges. The need for flexible programming based on modules and credit accumulation, opportunities to learn at any time through access to flexible learning centres, along with the accreditation of work-based learning and assessment on demand will all have to be met by colleges if they are to respond effectively to the growing demands of this category of worker.

- The changing nature of the working population: there are two major changes in the nature of the working population which will impact on colleges – the changes in age structure and gender mix.

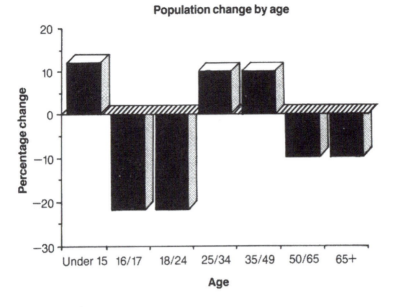

*Figure 2.3* Changes in age structure

Figure 2.3 illustrates the changes in the age structure of those in employment between now and the end of the century. It illustrates that during the 1990s the overall age of the working population will increase. More specifically the pressures for changes in the way colleges provide their services will result from the following factors:

♦ That 80 per cent of those already in employment will form the bulk of the workforce in the year 2000. The existing workforce will therefore bear the brunt of the technological changes needed to keep the country competitive. The retraining of this group will present a major challenge to colleges.

♦ That if more sixteen-year-olds enter full-time education, those available for employment at sixteen will decline significantly, or vice-versa. This age group represents the major client group for colleges and the current upturn in enrolments means colleges have switched most of their resources to providing for them. Reductions in take-up or changes in behaviour will therefore have a major impact on colleges.

♦ That by the end of the decade the number of workers between 35 and 55 will have increased by 10 per cent from 40 per cent of the workforce to around 50 per cent. Because of their statistical significance it is these workers who will be most directly affected by technological changes, thereby becoming potentially the major client group for re-training and accreditation.

In addition to changes in the age structure of the working population, changes in the gender mix will result in a marked move from male to female workers. This is evidenced by the fact that during the 1980s 85 per cent of the increase in the workforce was accounted for by women. This trend will continue during the 1990s to the point where 90 per cent of new jobs will be for women workers. Within this increase the proportion of women returners with children will increase faster than any other group. In order for them to take advantage of the opportunities available in further education, colleges will need to respond with a much more flexible approach to the timing of programmes and the variety of modes of study.

When this trend is linked with the increasing age structure of the workforce it means that the demand for college services will increasingly come from older clients, particularly women. This will mean that women, who already represent over 50 per cent of college enrolments, will become further education's most dominant client group.

## Opening up opportunities

In addition to the external pressures already mentioned there is a growing need for colleges to search for ways of opening up new opportunities for non-traditional groups to take up their services.

Satisfying this need requires the removal of barriers to access, acknowledging different cultural backgrounds, physical handicaps, individual circumstances, availability of time to study, economic status and any other circumstances which prevent attendance on traditional programmes of study.

# Chapter 3

# Teaching and learning frameworks

Most, if not all, colleges see their role in terms of providing learning opportunities which prepare individuals for their role in society and the world of employment.

As we move towards the environment of rapid change described in the last chapter colleges will increasingly have to search out ways of recognising that learning can and does take place in a variety of different situations. This recognition may result in colleges offering their services in two different yet overlapping areas:

1 Teaching and learning needs, focused on providing structured learning experiences, built around the recognition of different learning styles, offered through a wider variety of more open and flexible modes of delivery;
2 Assessment and accreditation needs, focused on recognising, assessing and accrediting achievements reached by individuals through their life- or work-based learning by experiences.

The two sets of needs overlap, but the extent of the overlap is unclear, and the size and extent of the client groups for each is difficult to assess. This makes it particularly difficult for colleges to plan the balance of their provision for each set of needs. As Figure 3.1 illustrates, what is seen of each set of needs may only be the tip of an iceberg with the true extent and shape of each hidden below the water-line.

This chapter deals with the frameworks needed to cater for teaching and learning needs. The next chapter will cover the responses to accreditation and assessment needs.

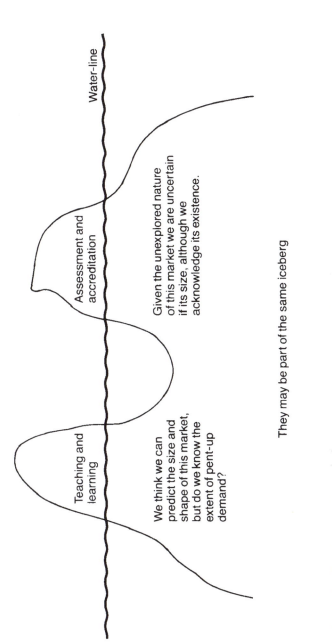

Water-line

Assessment and accreditation

Given the unexplored nature of this market we are uncertain if its size, although we acknowledge its existence.

Teaching and learning

We think we can predict the size and shape of this market, but do we know the extent of pent-up demand?

They may be part of the same iceberg

*Figure 3.1* Teaching and learning/assessment and accreditation

## TEACHING AND LEARNING: CATERING FOR CHANGING NEEDS

To ensure that the structured teaching and learning services offered by colleges stay relevant to the changing needs of individuals they will have to respond in four general ways:

- by paying attention to the current and future content relevance of their programmes
- by structuring their programmes so that they provide life-long learning opportunities
- by recognising and supporting alternative ways of learning and becoming accredited
- By responding to the increased expectations of their clients for greater access to and greater flexibility in the services offered.

### Future content relevance: the foundations for life-long learning

Ensuring that the content of all programmes offered meets today's needs and prepares individuals with the skills they will need to face change in the future is a major requirement of colleges. The amount of change which individuals will face during their lives requires that their initial education and training is based on three sets of content needs:

- to provide the skills and knowledge needed immediately to function effectively in today's social and working environment
- to develop transferable skills which can be used in new situations as they develop
- to establish a solid foundation of core skills which can be used as the platform for acquiring new skills and knowledge in the future as the need arises.

These three areas of need are inter-related rather than separate and therefore need to be acquired through an integrated programme of study and learning. Given the amount of change predicted, the key to the future lies in taking the long-term view of establishing a firm foundation of core skills, and not going for a short-term solution based on the immediate relevance of competences gained during initial education and training.

The inter-related elements of a foundation for life-long learning are illustrated in Figure 3.2, which illustrates the argument that the foundations for life-long learning need to be based on an inter-related approach which links initial job training with core and transferable skills. This linkage provides the platform for re-training in the future.

Expanding dimension of unknown needs

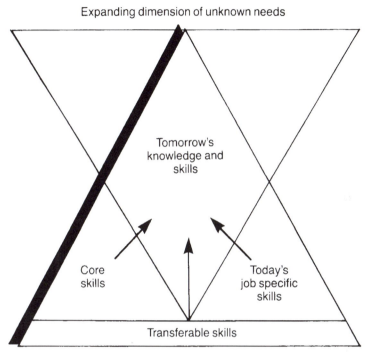

Base built on known need dimension

*Figure 3.2* The foundations of life-long learning

Although this approach is resisted by some who feel that the focus should be on today's needs, they are often the same people who claim that those they are recruiting lack basic skills.

Future employment and prosperity depend on equiping individuals with a firm base of core and transferable skills, such as:

- reading
- writing
- numeracy

- the ability to:
  - ◆ communicate effectively
  - ◆ use logic and reasoning in problem solving
- learning how to learn
- working alone, self-organisation, planning and time management
- working with others, team working, task and process skills.

These are the basic skills which will enable individuals to cope with change with confidence, and the belief that they can learn new skills as the need arises. However, they must also be provided with the opportunities to undertake life-long learning.

### Providing life-long learning opportunities

Supporting the move towards a learning society based on the opportunities for life-long learning through the development of open and flexible provision is the major challenge now facing colleges. It is already evident that the pace of change and its impact on employment patterns will require colleges to change the assumptions on which they prepare people for the world of employment.

In the past it was assumed that a good initial education and training would equip each individual with the knowledge and skills which, with a small amount of 'topping up', would sustain them through their adult lives. This established view of the usefulness of initial education/training is illustrated in Figure 3.3.

Despite its general acceptance it has always been recognised that different occupations would have different knowledge and skills profiles and different demands for 'top up' training, depending on the nature of the occupation and its vulnerability to the pace of change.

It can no longer be assumed that initial training will sustain individuals through their working life. Indeed, the useful life of much initial training will quickly diminish. This is particularly true in rapid-moving technologies, where advances need supporting with the up-skilling of workers. In these situations the usefulness of initial training needs to be viewed within the context of Figure 3.4, which illustrates the amount of retraining needed in some technologies in order to sustain employment.

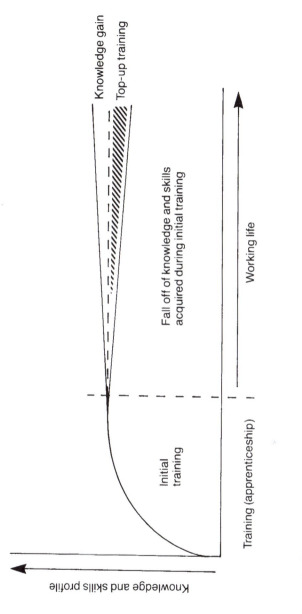

*Figure 3.3* The established view of initial knowledge and skills fall-off

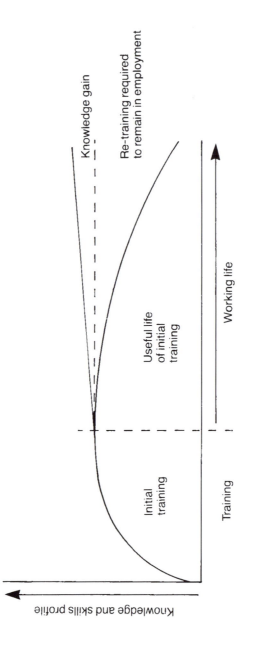

Figure 3.4 Amount of re-training now required for jobs in fast-moving technologies

Life-long learning and training opportunities now need developing, particularly for those areas of employment facing rapid change. In future these areas of employment will need to be viewed in terms of a continuum of overlapping, short-lived, steady states of knowledge and skills which will require continual up-dating if the individual is to sustain employment. Figure 3.5 illustrates this view of the need to continually update skills and knowledge, throughout the working life.

Each circle in the diagram represents workers' job knowledge and skills requirements at various points throughout their working lives.

The impact of providing for life-long learning will require colleges to think of new ways of providing services more flexibly through modularisation of learning and assessment of their structured programmes, the provision of flexible open access learning centres, individualised learning agreements and partnership schemes. They will also need to recognise alternative ways of learning other than by structured programmes, including the accreditation of work-based learning through assessment on demand and the accreditation of prior learning.

### Structuring programmes into modular frameworks/credit accumulation

Arranging the curriculum into a modular framework can offer many advantages to the learner. However, if the balance between coherence and flexibility is to be achieved, a college must be clear about:

- its reasons for moving towards a fully modularised programme
- what it means by modularisation, and its definition and use of the term module
- having a shared vision about how to manage and deliver the modular programmes
- the additional systems and services it will need to support its modular programme.

All of these aspects must be thought about and synchronised, together with appropriate systems and staff development, if modularisation is to be a success.

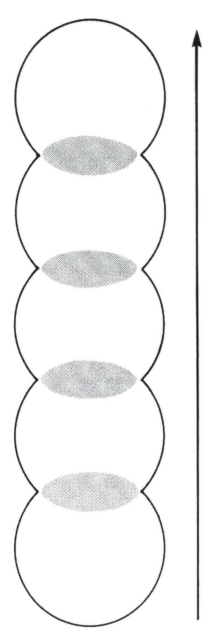

Working life

*Figure 3.5* Working life seen as a continuum of skills and knowledge

The arguments for moving towards modularisation of the programmes are generally based on the following:

- Modular frameworks open up access by allowing individual students to negotiate programmes of study which best meet their individual needs. Assessment and accreditation can also be matched to the needs of individuals.
- The frameworks allow for single modules or combinations of modules to be arranged to meet the specific needs of individuals.
- Programmes can also be put together based on single or combinations of different modes of study, i.e. structured study programmes, flexible learning, partnerships with employers linked to work-based learning, accreditation of prior learning or assessment on demand.
- Programmes can be arranged to meet the needs of full-time students, whilst at the same time enabling other students to take the same programme at their own pace by controlling the timing and method of study used.
- Individuals can progress more quickly through a modular scheme due to opportunities to claim exemption or credit through the accreditation of prior learning.
- By monitoring the progress of individuals carefully it is possible to review the modules being taken by the learner and combine them in ways which give greater progress and thereby reduce the likelihood of drop out.
- Modularisation provides the opportunity for credit accumulation over different time periods within one defined framework. It also enables separate modules to be taken for specific purposes such as re-training or updating.
- Carefully structured modular frameworks will avoid repetition in programme content and assessment by avoiding the duplication of common competences located in different occupational or subject areas.

These lines of argument combine to offer a modular framework which can offer comprehensive programmes of study to meet the needs of individuals of any age. They open up access and provide a responsive service which can be tailored to individual circumstances. At the same time the framework can be negotiated by using single or a combination of modes of study, including work-based learning and the accreditation of prior learning. Therefore, despite the problems of organising and managing such a framework, it is likely to offer the best opportunities to provide comprehensive opportunities for all learners.

### Recognising and supporting alternative ways of learning

Given these obvious advantages one is forced to ask why such a system has not yet been fully implemented. The problem lies in defining what is meant by the term module, which means different things to different people and must therefore be used carefully. There is no shared and accepted use of the word, which makes the design of a module difficult to achieve. The list below shows the areas of confusion and lack of concensus on which to build a common modular framework.

- Does it mean a module of assessment or a module of learning?
- Is the term being used to describe:
  - a set of outcomes contributing to a specific award?
  - a set of process skills?
  - a range of prescribed or described learning activities?
  - a schedule of learning outcomes in the form of competence statements?
  - a content list of knowledge and skills?
  - a period of study time, usually in hours?

The confusion must be removed if progress is to be made and the introduction of National Vocational Qualifications, in the form of competence-based statements, along with the modular structure of General Vocational Qualifications, is to offer a positive way forward. This will provide a framework around which the modular provision can be developed.

Such a framework will need the support of the following:

- guidance services based on individual needs
- assessment services
- progression planning
- individual action planning
- facilities and systems for assessing and awarding accreditation for prior learning
- partnership arrangements to cover work-based learning
- student tracking services linked to systems for recording credit accumulation

- special support modules such as study skills, self-management, assessment procedures
- alternative modes for delivery modules such as structured programmes, flexible timetables, flexible learning provision, individualised study arrangements, partnership schemes, and so on.

When all these are in place the framework will truly meet the needs of individuals and be accessible to all.

## Provision of flexible open access learning centres

The area of flexible learning is already becoming well established in colleges and will increasingly become a much more important component of college provision. Existing provision will develop quickly as the rapid pace of development is implemented within colleges. This will enable them to extend their learning opportunities beyond the modular programmes described earlier to include the availability of these modules along with tutor support in the form of self-study programmes in well resourced study centres. The development will not only offer a choice between structured programmes and flexible learning, it will also facilitate integration between all the options available to open up learning. Some examples of this are:

- structured curriculum programme only
- flexible learning centre programme only
- a combination of both
- individualised learning plan using a combination of both plus other options
- partnership schemes, including different modes of study through individual study and work-based learning linked into modular programmes with learning centre 'top up'
- learning networks linking different modes of study with different agencies.

The function of learning centres is to provide a more flexible service to learners which will enable them to:

- determine their own learning objectives and the pace at which they learn
- provide tutor support to aid their learning progress

- offer testing and assessment services which will enable learners to gauge their progress or claim accreditation
- offer a record-keeping service to students who wish to claim accreditation at some point in the future.

The developing technology associated with learning centres will allow for their multiple use. Colleges will move away from concepts of using flexible learning workshops for one main purpose, such as providing back-up support to learners on structured programmes of study or open learning, towards multi-media, multi-use arrangements.

Colleges will need to determine their own strategy for developing these centres either in a geographically dispersed way (small, specialist centres dispersed throughout a college) or in large, centrally organised areas aimed at providing specialist staffing and economies of scale. The architectural constraints inherited from the design of yesterday's colleges will have a major influence on the strategies adopted.

### Individual learning agreements

The prospect of modularisation and credit transfer creates the possibility of introducing individualised learning agreements. These agreements will open up education to individuals in a way which will allow them to personalise the content, timing and pace of their learning. Such agreements will be very different from many of the learning contracts currently offered by colleges, which often restrict the agreement to the rules and procedures to be followed by each party during the learning process.

Individualised learning agreements focus on the specific needs of each learner and enable him or her to answer the following key questions:

- What are my learning objectives?
- What do I need to learn and why?
- What style of learning suits me best?
- What learning activities do I need to engage in to meet my needs?
- What resources will I need to use to achieve my learning?
- What are the best methods for satisfying my needs: structured learning, flexible learning centre, open learning, work-based learning and so on?

* Through what agency can I best put my learning package together?

The learner will need guidance and support to answer these questions but, once answered, the key question of the best agency to put the package together becomes paramount. Many colleges will provide this service of individualised learning through the medium of learning agreements. As the agreement will also serve as the learning plan for the individual concerned it will need to be very specific in terms of defining:

* the purposes of the agreement for both parties
* what period the agreement will cover
* what costs the learner has to meet
* the learning outcomes to be achieved, preferably in objective form
* what learning styles will be made available
* methods to be used for learning and assessment

    ♦ How will the learning be done?
    ♦ How will its outcomes be assessed?

* what resources the learner will be able to call on during the period covered by the agreement
* how the evaluation will be carried out by both parties.

Individualised learning linked to modularisation and credit accumulation will, when co-ordinated within partnership schemes and learning networks, offer great flexibility to potential learners, and enable them to put together packages of learning which meet their own specific needs.

*Partnership schemes*

Resulting from the recognition that learning takes place in a variety of situations, the next decade will see the growth of partnership schemes between individuals, colleges and employers. The formal linkage of these interests will ensure that the learning needs of individuals are met through the joint efforts of all partners involved. Figure 3.6 illustrates the bringing together of an individual, an employer and a college into a three-way partnership agreement.

Such agreements bring together in a planned way the learning opportunities available through individual study, work-based

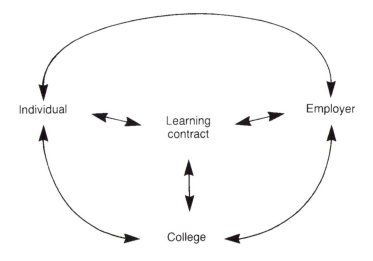

*Figure 3.6* Three-way partnership agreement

learning and college provision. The responsibilities of each party are stated in the agreement, along with the methods of assessment and accreditation. The use of training log books and records of achievement are usually included in the formal arrangements set out in the agreement to the scheme.

In the case of work-based learning there may be a requirement for more than one employer to be involved. This may be particularly necessary where a wide range of work-based competences are required which cannot be provided by a single employer.

There are three main reasons why partnership schemes will continue to become more important:

1 Because of the need to provide for the training and re-training needs of workers in an integrated way. This is especially true for knowledge workers operating in fast-moving technologies.
2 Because many colleges will not be able to keep pace with some of the changes in employment needs, nor be able to match the investment required to keep up-to-date and provide for technological/hardware/software developments.
3 Because time pressures will require a sharing of responsibilities. The result of this may well be that colleges will have to become more active in the areas of assessment of work-based learning and accreditation of prior learning.

Partnership schemes can be linked together through the use of learning agreements between all parties involved. In bringing them together partnership schemes recognise the need to provide a range of different learning experiences. Some of these experiences will be provided by all the parties working together, or by a combination of different experiences provided by different partners. Partnership schemes will lead eventually to the full integration of employers' training and work-based learning with colleges programmes. They will also lead to the development of new services such as assessment on demand and the accreditation of prior learning.

*Learning networks*

Building on the notion of partnership schemes is the idea of extending them to form learning networks, which will be based on access and progression routes, supported by credit accumulation for individuals. This will enable them to match the available opportunities for learning to their own personal needs. Learning networks also recognise that because of the growing complexity in the needs of individuals, colleges on their own may not be able to provide a full and flexible set of quality opportunities for all those who approach them.

The development of learning networks will enable colleges to provide for a wider range of needs. They may be formed by establishing links with universities, institutes of higher education, other colleges, schools, training and enterprise councils, industrial and commercial concerns, public services and, where appropriate, private providers. They may also be arranged to complement a college's own core business, adding to it by providing access progression and credit accumulation opportunities. The college's own core business may in this way be extended by franchising both outwards to schools and colleges and inwards through links with universities and colleges of higher education. Learning networks increase the opportunities for life-long learning by:

- giving wider access to learning opportunities
- providing access to different levels of award
- providing progression pathways and credit accumulation
- giving equal value to all the ways and situations in which learning can and does take place
- awarding accreditation for different ways of learning

- allowing for the recognition of achievement through accepted and recognised standards of awards
- increasing co-operation and understanding between all parties involved in the network
- opening up more opportunities for individual learners.

Figure 3.7 illustrates the parties who may be involved in a learning network. Each network will be different, depending on the parties involved and the needs of the learner.

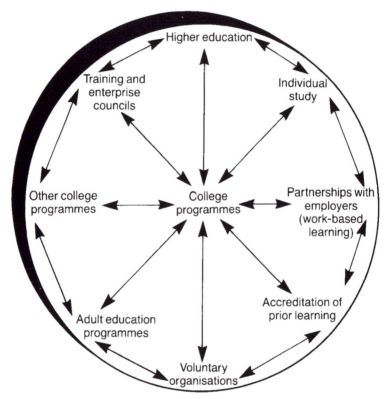

*Figure 3.7* Illustration of a learning network

*Equal value*

For such networks to work effectively they must be based on the notion of equal value. This means that all the ways in which individuals can achieve a recognised outcome must be treated as equal. For example, accreditation of prior learning must be treated as being of equal value to traditional teaching and learning. This notion of equal value must be reflected in the physical and human resources provided to support each of the routes to achievement available within the learning network.

*Increased expectations*

The future impact on colleges of delivering life-long learning opportunities could well be felt in demands for even more sophisticated systems of teaching and learning based on information technology coupled with interactive learning systems. There will also be pressure for this to be backed up by customised services delivered flexibly to meet these expectations. This flexibility will need to build around the acceptance by colleges that individuals will arrive with different needs in the form of:

- preferred learning styles
- time pressures
- individual circumstances
- ethnic/cultural traditions
- expectations
- funding/support arrangements.

Of particular importance will be the response from colleges to support the larger number of adults, particularly women, who will be wanting to use their services. Flexibility in attendance and child care facilities are particular areas in which colleges will have to improve their performance over the next decade, because these individuals will require:

- information on which to base decisions
- advice and guidance
- action planning/scheduling
- clear progression opportunities
- recognition of past achievements
- award recording
- flexibility of options
- learning contracts specifying partnership arrangements
- support services such as counselling and child care facilities.

These needs can be arranged into three services which colleges will need to provide, and which are illustrated in Figure 3.8.

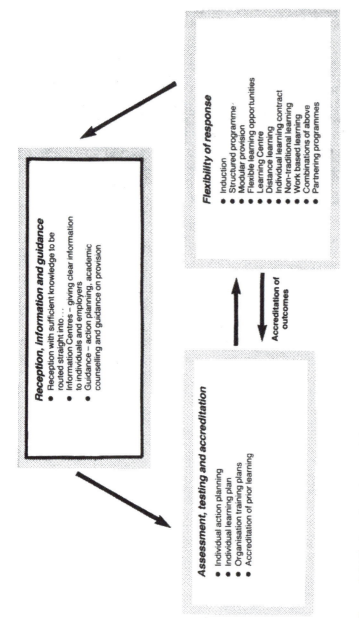

**Reception, information and guidance**
- Reception with sufficient knowledge to be routed straight into . . .
- Information Centres — giving clear information to individuals and employers
- Guidance — action planning, academic counselling and guidance on provision

**Flexibility of response**
- Induction
- Structured programme
- Modular provision
- Flexible learning opportunities
- Learning Centre
- Distance learning
- Individual learning contract
- Non-traditional learning
- Work based learning
- Combinations of above
- Partnering programmes

**Assessment, testing and accreditation**
- Individual action planning
- Individual learning plan
- Organisation training plans
- Accreditation of prior learning

Accreditation of outcomes

*Figure 3.8* Life-long learning model

# Chapter 4

# Accreditation and assessment services

Accreditation of prior learning is based on the recognition that learning takes place in a wide variety of real life situations. By accepting this the learning is credited as being of equal value to that gained in more traditional teaching and learning situations. The processes associated with accreditation provide opportunities for formally recognising and accrediting all learning no matter where it takes place.

## THE RECOGNITION OF PRIOR LEARNING

To the individuals concerned the process of formally valuing and recognising their learning:

- boosts their confidence by formally recognising and valuing their past achievements, thereby providing an opportunity to enhance their self-esteem and motivate them towards further learning;
- provides a more flexible and open route to the recognition of their achievements within an open framework of equal opportunities;
- accelerates the possible recognition of achievements, thereby providing the potential to save time by awarding full or partial exemptions from recognised awards;
- widens the potential opportunities of gaining access to:

  - further/higher education/training
  - paid or unpaid employment

- provides an opportunity to

  - undertake or evaluate a career review
  - plan a career change
  - alter an existing career direction

• provides a platform and framework for personal action planning.

## Opportunities provided by the accreditation process

Accreditation of prior learning provides an open framework which can be used for a variety of purposes. This provides for the flexibility of outcomes resulting from its uses, which can be seen in Figure 4.1.

### The accreditation framework

At its simplest, the framework for accrediting prior learning requires the college to manage the candidate's progress through the stages shown in Figure 4.2.

Most awarding bodies outline their own requirements for the process involved in the accreditation of prior learning of which the National Council for Vocational Qualifications (NCVQ) sets out the framework shown in Figure 4.3.

Each stage requires the college to take the candidate for accreditation through a carefully thought through process, designed to ensure their success. This process is illustrated in Figure 4.4.

### Pre-entry

Upon contacting the college, prospective APL candidates receive information about the APL process, the opportunities it presents to them and the costs and time involved. If they wish to proceed they complete an information/application form which starts the process of accreditation.

### Initial interview

At this stage the processes are outlined which enable prospective candidates to identify and review their experiential learning. This is usually done either in a workshop setting or on a one-to-one basis with a specialist APL counsellor.

The outcome of this stage is usually an action plan enabling the candidate to map out how they will collect and present the evidence required for accreditation.

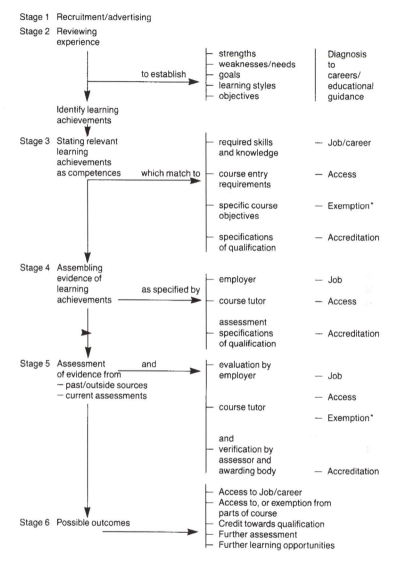

*applies only when allowed by some awarding bodies

*Figure 4.1* APL for different purposes
*Source*: Reproduced from the Assessment of Prior Learning and Learner Services by permission of the FEU

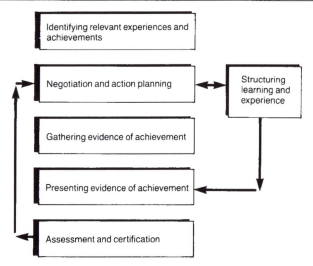

*Figure 4.2* Stages in the APL process

Gathering and presenting evidence of prior learning

It is during this stage that candidates work either on their own in workshops, or with the help of a supervisor to collect and generate the evidence which will be used to assess their prior learning.

The evidence generated forms the basis of the candidate's assessment portfolio. In the APL context, this portfolio is an organised presentation of information on past experiences and accomplishments. It may also include evidence from employers or other authoritative sources that the candidate has reliably and consistently demonstrated skills, knowledge and/or understanding which can be used to gain recognition of credit. Candidates need skilled help during this stage to ensure that their presented portfolios are relevant, concise and presented in a way which enables credit to be claimed.

Assessment

During assessment a specialist subject assessor reviews the candidate's portfolio and agrees a further assessment if necessary.

Assessment can take a variety of different forms appropriate to the needs of the learning being accredited. These can include oral questioning, simulations, demonstrations, work shadowing, or any other form of valid and reliable assessment which may help

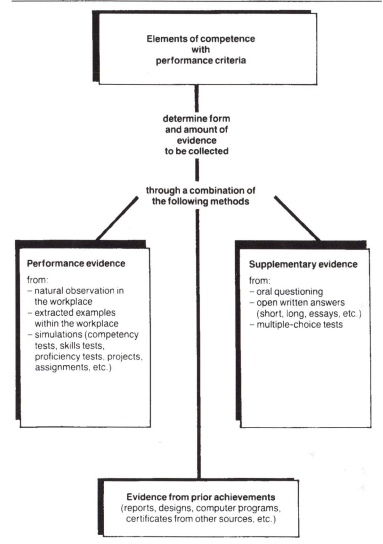

*Figure 4.3* Stages in the APL process as defined by NCVQ

the specialist subject assessor to validate the candidate's claim for accreditation.

Effective assessment forms the basis of accreditation and needs to be carried out carefully and consistently if the process is to maintain credibility.

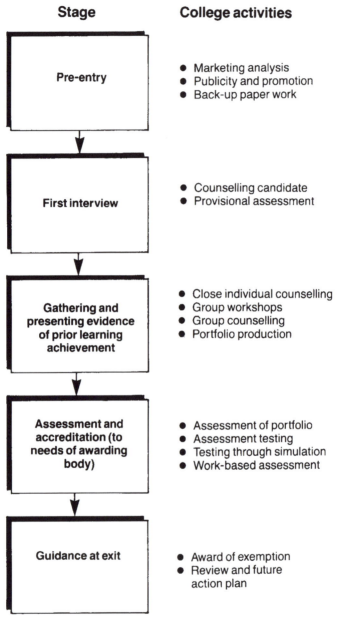

**Stage**                    **College activities**

Pre-entry
- Marketing analysis
- Publicity and promotion
- Back-up paper work

First interview
- Counselling candidate
- Provisional assessment

Gathering and presenting evidence of prior learning achievement
- Close individual counselling
- Group workshops
- Group counselling
- Portfolio production

Assessment and accreditation (to needs of awarding body)
- Assessment of portfolio
- Assessment testing
- Testing through simulation
- Work-based assessment

Guidance at exit
- Award of exemption
- Review and future action plan

*Figure 4.4* The APL process

**Accreditation**  If the assessment proves positive and the candidate is recommended for accreditation, an awarding body representative will be asked to review the evidence used in assessment and, assuming a positive review, the award of a credit will be approved.

Exit guidance

The final stage of the process involves reviewing the outcomes of assessment with the candidates and helping them to draw up action plans for the next stage of their development.

*Integrating the process*

To operate effectively all the stages involved in the accreditation process must be fully integrated and supported by appropriate systems and resources. The outline for this integration is shown in Figure 4.5.

## ASSESSMENT ON DEMAND SERVICES

The use of accreditation of prior learning and the recognition of work-based learning when linked to the rights to assessment on demand required in National Vocational Qualification programmes, require the establishment of assessment centre services.

When established, these centres will offer either open or scheduled assessment services under the strict controls needed to safeguard standards and ensure equity of treatment to all those being assessed. Centres will therefore be managed by trained staff who offer assessment under controlled conditions. The size of the centres and hours of operation will be determined by the level of demand and access requirements.

In general terms the centres will offer two broad categories of assessment services:

1  Initial/diagnostic assessments, which are aimed at enabling individuals to succeed in their chosen areas of study or to claim exemption through accreditation for parts of the programme. Assessments will therefore be designed to give credit or establish starting points for study through a combination of the following:

| Stage | Tutor activity | Candidate activity | Documentation |
|---|---|---|---|
| Top up learning | Arranges top up learning as appropriate to complete unit claims (plus related assessment) | Undertakes top up learning and related assessment as appropriate | |
| | Completes unit record of evidence | All evidence in portfolio organised to correlate with unit of evidence categories | |
| | Arranges verification and moderation with awarding body | | |
| Outcomes: Accreditation Further assessment | Arranges further assessments | Receives unit credits Undertakes further assessments | |
| Further learning | Offers guidance on how to achieve credit for further units/full awards, e.g. work-based learning, self study, college-based units | Undertakes further learning | |

*Figure 4.5* Stages in the integration of the APL process

*Source*: Based on MCI guidelines/BTEC APL guidelines/NCVQ Staff Development Pack; Accreditation of PLA. Reproduced from the Assessment of Prior Learning and Learner Services by permission of the FEU

(a) establishing starting levels of learning achievement and supporting necessary requirements

(b) identifying preferred learning styles and matching them to study methods available e.g. structured programmes, flexible learning centres, open learning, accreditation, etc.

(c) giving credit for previous achievement and exemption of study programmes

(d) selecting the learning method which best suits the needs of the individual concerned

2  Assessment of programme standards or progress made: the centre's main work will be offering assessment services to the college's programmes of study, through main-line study programmes, flexible learning centres or work-based learning partnerships. Tests will be subject to strict security and quality control criteria and will be available either on demand (i.e. through candidates presenting themselves and satisfying the identity criteria) or at pre-determined scheduled times, depending on the level of demand, the nature of the test and the security demanded to ensure that standards are met.

Centres will also offer re-testing services designed to enable students to keep up with the requirements of their study programmes.

## Accreditation of work-based learning

The recognition that learning can and does take place in a wide variety of situations will, when linked to finding additional ways of recognising the accreditation needs of those already in employment, move tomorrow's colleges further towards the recognition and accreditation of work-based learning. The framework for achieving this will involve colleges in:

• identifying and specifying the competences which it can assess and recognise within the guidelines of the various validating bodies

• setting up frameworks which allow individuals and their employers to plan a work-based learning programme and its accreditation

• helping individuals to establish their learning programme and the mentor support network needed to support it and collect the evidence required for assessment and accreditation

- arranging for the work-based assessment to take place within the actual working environment or off-site within the college's assessment unit
- checking the outcome of the assessment with the internal verifier
- completing the verification process with the awarding body's verifier
- arranging for the necessary accreditation/certification to take place.

The parties involved in the process of the accreditation of work-based learning are shown in Figure 4.6.

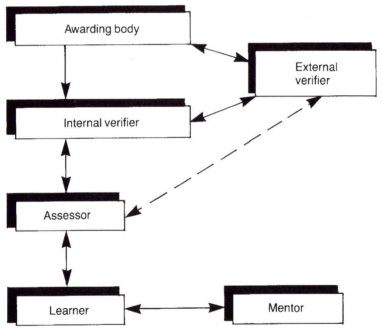

*Figure 4.6* Parties involved in the accreditation of work-based learning

*Learners*

At the centre of the work-based learning process are the learners, whose role is that of setting learning goals and, with the help of their mentor, planning progress towards them. During the actual learning process learners are proactive, through the process of self-assessment, in measuring their progress and the extra support which they may need to achieve their learning goals. To do this effectively they must be able to fully understand the assessment guidelines and methods by which they will be able to judge their performance. Providing they have been effectively inducted into the requirements of their programme and have a firm grasp of the competences they are required to achieve they should soon be able to self-evaluate their progress. This element of self-evaluation is important in learning how to organise a learning programme and assess their own progress as learners.

## Work-based mentors

The work-based mentor's role is that of supporting learners and assisting them to reach the standards of performance required by the assessors. Mentors are therefore key people in the work-based learning process and their learner support and guidance role can be a major factor in the learners' success. The mentor must be kept separate from, and independent of, the assessment process, and should take the role of friend and supporter to the learner. For this reason the role is best undertaken by someone outside the learners' line management or supervisory framework if it is to be seen as non-threatening support and guidance.

## Work-based assessors

The actual assessment of learners' ability to satisfy the requirements of the competences being aimed for is undertaken by work-based assessors, whose role is that of assessing performance against the standards set out in the range of performance competences required to be met for accreditation.

To satisfy the requirements of their role assessors need to be vocationally competent and very clear about the standards of performance required from the learner. Consistency of judgement by assessors is ensured through their assessment by internal verifiers.

## Internal verifiers

It is the responsibility of internal verifiers to monitor the consistency of assessments made by work-based assessors. In turn, their verifications are sampled and reviewed by the awarding body's verifiers with the aim of ensuring the consistency and reliability of assessments of the learners. The role of the internal verifier is therefore linked into the co-ordinating and quality control role of the awarding body's own verifier.

### Awarding body's verifiers

Each awarding body carries the responsibility for monitoring and evaluating for accreditation the work of the work-based assessors. It is their responsibility to ensure that their guidelines have been effectively implemented and the standards of competence required have been properly assessed and accredited. The credibility of the accreditation of work-based learning therefore depends on the effectiveness of the verification process. It is also the responsibility of each awarding body to ensure the following three key elements of accreditation are in place:

- a quality control system which ensures that the sampling methods used for assessment are valid, consistent and reliable
- an effective framework for both the assessment methods and the verification of assessment standards
- that accreditation is followed through to the recording and certification of successful candidates.

These functions are carried out by the awarding body's own verifier whose role is to check on the work of the internal verifiers and assessors to ensure that their judgements are consistent and meet the requirements of published guidelines for the accreditation of work-based learning.

# Chapter 5

# The shape of tomorrow's colleges

The moves towards greater flexibility and responsiveness in teaching and learning and accreditation and assessment described in chapters three and four begin to frame the emerging shape of tomorrow's colleges. By bringing them together, it is possible to map out the developments needed to shape tomorrow's colleges.

These factors can be brought together as appropriate to the needs of each college, to form the building blocks of future development. The blocks can be rearranged as required to suit the particular staff expertise of the college and the needs of the markets it serves as shown in Figure 5.2.

## CHARACTERISTICS OF TOMORROW'S COLLEGES

Tomorrow's colleges will be developed by their managements as they face the pressures for change and respond to them in line with the needs of the communities and industrial/commercial industries they serve. They will be built around flexibility of response, open access and accreditation of alternative ways of learning. They are likely to have the following characteristics:

- Structure: a menu of alternative learning and accreditation opportunities based on:

  ♦ individualised learning based on modular programmes which allow individuals to 'pick and mix' their activities to meet their own particular needs
  ♦ bespoke study opportunities
  ♦ individualised, student-centred learning
  ♦ flexible modes of delivery through structured programmes,

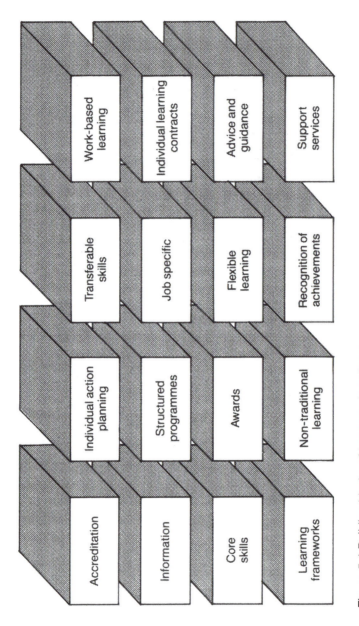

*Figure 5.1* Building blocks of tomorrow's colleges

The building blocks shown in the figure:

| | | | |
|---|---|---|---|
| Work-based learning | Individual learning contracts | Advice and guidance | Support services |
| Transferable skills | Job specific | Flexible learning | Recognition of achievements |
| Individual action planning | Structured programmes | Awards | Non-traditional learning |
| Accreditation | Information | Core skills | Learning frameworks |

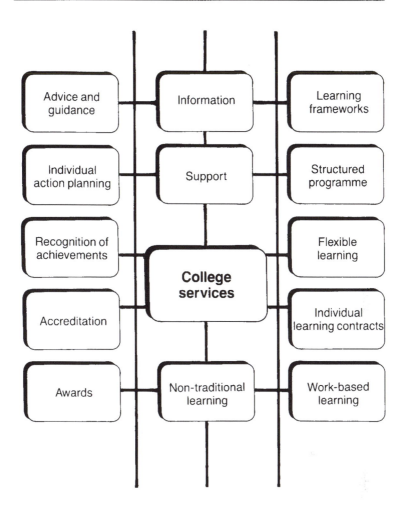

*Figure 5.2* Map of education and training developments

learning centres, open learning, partnership agreements and personalised learning contracts
♦ continuous enrolment throughout the year onto roll on/roll off programmes
• Support systems: the outcome of these learning and accreditation structures will be a change in the way college buildings are laid out and arranged to provide:

- ♦ information and admissions units
- ♦ flexible scheduling of resources and study accreditation opportunities
- ♦ resource-based learning
- ♦ increased access support for students with specific educational needs
- ♦ increased child care facilities
- ♦ student-centred admissions systems
- ♦ high profile student services

- Management systems: resulting from the above, colleges will need to develop new ways of measuring efficiency and effectiveness, which take into account and place equal value on all the ways in which individuals can achieve accreditation for learning. These will include resource target-setting and monitoring based on key indicators of flexibility and student progress and the ability to track students through all the pathways to accreditation and allow them to accumulate credit.

The relationship between these characteristics is shown in Figure 5.3.

### Openness and accessibility

In addition to the characteristics which have just been described, tomorrow's colleges will need to assess their degree of openness and accessibility by developing some form of index. This will need to measure the different ways of being a student or of achieving a recognised award or measure of accreditation. Each part of the college's programme should then be assessed using the index to identify the need for developments to improve openness and accessibility.

The index could be based on a single mode or a combination of different modes, such as:

- full-time study
- a variety of part-time combinations
- a flexible learning centre programme
- distance or open learning
- a roll on/roll off basis
- assessment on demand
- accreditation of prior learning

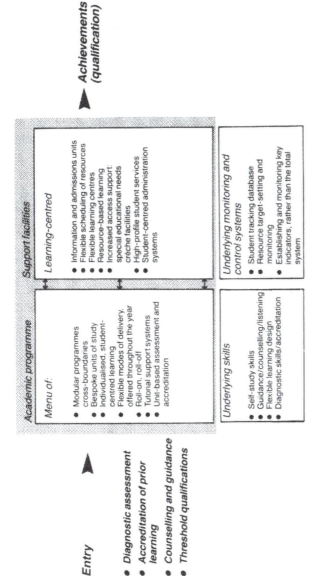

*Figure 5.3* Tomorrow's colleges: providers of achievement-based qualifications

- work-based learning
- accreditation of employers' training
- non-traditional learning.

It is only when each and every award offered by the college can be achieved singly or by combinations of most, if not all, of the routes set out above that true openness and flexibility will be available to potential students.

### Strategic issues

Colleges will need to consider the following strategic issues which relate to developing tomorrow's colleges:

- growing demands for education/training
- increased demand for flexibility and the provision of more open/accessible opportunities
- a growing number of more discriminating students who will wish to have clearer agreements with the college based on the acknowledgement of the rights and responsibilities of both parties.
- shorter lead times and quicker responses to new education/training packages
- recognition of work-based and non-traditional modes of learning and achieving, including accreditation and assessment on demand
- pressures on funding resulting in lower unit-costs and least-cost provision
- protection of the core business of teaching and learning balanced by flexible learning centres, guidance and assessment
- funding of national targets, which may reduce local responsiveness and freedom of action
- that becoming an independent corporation will, in the short term, mean a shift to financial management and information systems being the main focus
- maintaining and improving quality
- coping creatively with the pressures resulting from increased demand and a stable or declining resource base
- responding positively and imaginatively to the pressures for growth
- increasing flexibility, access and choice

- developing a network of learning and achievement opportunities with other providers
- developing a learning organisation which can reshape itself to:
  - ♦ meet changing needs
  - ♦ accept that mistakes are inevitable when dealing with uncertainty and change
  - ♦ locate decision-making and responsibility as close as possible to the point of action
  - ♦ maintain and encourage the college's change culture.

The strategic trick will be that of balancing:

- increased demand
- declining resources, while
  - ♦ maintaining quality of choice and experience.

# Chapter 6

# Developing a distinct mission for the college

## CREATING A VISION

In moving into the future and formulating the college's response to change, it is necessary to develop a clear mission statement to guide its planning. This mission should be based on a vision of the future and what the college feels it can achieve. There are two broad approaches towards creating a vision of the future:

1 Some kind of logical analysis of existing circumstances matched against opportunities for the future. There are a variety of rationally focused models which colleges can use to undertake this form of analysis.
2 The creation of a more intuitive vision of a possible future based on the notion that such a future can be aimed for and realised through positive action.

In these days of discontinuous change it is more difficult than in the past to apply the first approach with any degree of reliability. The second approach sees the vision as a mental journey from the known to the unknown in order to create a future from current facts, to which are added the hopes, dreams, opportunities and dangers surrounding the present situation. If this approach is adopted it must be set within a disciplined framework based on:

- continually searching for new ideas, concepts and ways of thinking which enable the vision of the future to take a clear shape
- being able to articulate clearly this vision in ways which enable it to be communicated and integrated into a philosophy which can then be applied to provide a clear sense of mission to guide the strategic direction of the college

- being able to translate the vision and mission in ways which are meaningful to staff to the point where they are happy to support them
- being able to assess the success of the college in terms of its ability to travel towards and achieve its vision.

The vision put forward in this book is one which sees colleges adding to their existing core business the much wider accreditation of non-traditional ways of learning, providing assessment on demand, modular 'pick and mix' programmes based either in colleges or in partnerships with employers and other organisations. In such a vision the business of colleges moves away from providing courses and pathways to qualifications, towards enabling individuals to achieve their personal goals through a variety of opportunities, each of which meets their own personal needs.

This kind of vision is not arrived at through analysis of what already exists but by extrapolating existing trends into the future. It is a vision of what could be if we removed some of the barriers which stand in the way of true openness and accessibility. It places the successful achievement of individual needs above the protection of the status quo. Because it challenges the status quo it is seen by some both as irrational and as too demanding of existing staff and established college systems. However, it is a vision which generates considerable passion and a determination to follow it through to success.

### Converting the vision into a mission for the college

The insistence by the new Further Education Funding Council that each college in the sector must have a clear statement of mission raises its importance as a strategic management tool. This challenges colleges to be clear about stating their vision, direction, purpose and values.

If done effectively, each mission statement should convey the character, identity and reasons for the college's existence. Within this context, key questions to be faced are:

- Should the college depart radically from its traditional role by moving from a service to a business regime?
- Should it continue to meet the needs of its traditional community, concentrating on providing comprehensively for all those needs or only for defined sectors?

Each college must clarify its own role and purpose by answering these questions for itself. However, in moving forward it is wiser for each new mission statement to grow out of the college's traditions, for it is well to remember that radical departures from the past often fail, because it is forgotten that the new mission has to appeal to those segments of the population which have traditionally supported the college.

*Establishing starting points*

A good starting point to establish the true characteristics of a college is to consider a period of time, say the last five years, and ask:

- What sort of students have actually enrolled, remained and qualified?
- What kinds of staff accepted appointments?
- What kinds of staff turned down offers and why?
- What kinds of staff tend to stay for a long time?
- How do ex-students see the value of attendance at college?
- What other people contribute to the institution (i.e. sponsors), and for what reasons?

The analysis will need to be interpreted with great care, as slavish adherence to the past would be foolish, but to disregard the past would be even more unwise.

The conclusion to the analysis should be the answer to the question: 'What is the essence of this college?'

Finally, as stated earlier, the new, distinctive role and mission must be rooted in the college's traditions and appeal to traditional supporters. Radical departures from the past student base most frequently fail; building on is the best approach.

Those in senior management positions must have a clear notion of what they want to achieve, the ability to communicate their ideas to others and the determination to diminish the impact of those who might subvert the achievement of these ideas.

It is frequently argued that a college's strength and ability to survive result from a diversity of opinions and the freedom to dissent. However, there are times when unanimous support is essential and the development of a new mission may be one of them. Those who cannot embrace the college's new role should leave rather than jeopardise its chances of success.

When one examines those colleges which have made major successful changes, it is found, almost invariably, that those who strongly opposed the changes have been replaced.

*Developing a sense of mission*

A sense of mission is only truly created when there is an attachment between individual members of staff and the college. This sense of commitment can be enhanced through the process of clarifying the mission. However, because few colleges are explicit about their values, individuals are left to sense them out by observing the behaviour of other members of the organisation.

For example, if the behaviour standards are about a student-centred approach to learning, members of staff will be able to sense this through the general approach of colleagues towards their work. This is reinforced by the activities supported by managers. The stronger the match between college policies and individual values, the greater will be each individual's commitment to the college's mission.

A sense of mission therefore originates from the closeness of the values match, because it is at the level of values that staff become emotionally committed to the college and its stated mission. This raises real issues about ownership of college missions. The 1992 Further and Higher Education Act placed the responsibility for formulating a college's mission with the governing bodies. The problem with this is one of staff ownership and commitment. Most governing bodies will take a lead in their responsibility from college management and this may present an opportunity for dealing with the issue of ownership.

Starting with a clear concept of ownership is therefore important. Is the college's mission that of:

- the governors, who have the responsibility of defining it under the Further and Higher Education Act?
- the managers, whose role it is to translate the mission into plans and action?
- the staff, who will have to identify with and share the mission if it is to be fully translated into reality?

Clearly, all of the above must share the college's mission if it is to be a success, but it is most important that there should be staff ownership.

Benefits of staff ownership

The benefits to the college of having staff who share its mission and its underpinning values are:

- better decision-making, clearer communications and more effective delegation, linked to less need for close supervision.
- loyalty and commitment to the college's overall direction
- colleges with clear values find it easier to recruit, select, promote and develop their staff
- individuals who do not agree with the organisation's values can and do decide to leave
- staff with a sense of mission find it easier to work together, and to respect and trust one another.

*Expectations of interest groups (stakeholders)*

In defining its mission the college must take into account the expectations of the various groups who are interested in the way it behaves and structures its services.

These groups represent much wider interests than those who actually consume the college's services. They include: the funding bodies, the community at large, the governing body, customers, the college's staff, external validating/examining bodies and other external bodies. These interests must be taken into account when shaping the college's general mission statement.

Colleges are social institutions and as such a much wider public than those who directly work in them or take up their services have an interest in their activities. These are known collectively as the college stakeholders. The successful college must take account of these wider interests and expectations when planning its activities.

For example, an analysis of the expectations of stakeholders for a particular college may include the following:

| | |
|---|---|
| Customers/students | Employment, qualifications, social facilities, range of provision to meet aspirations, information, counselling and access, equal opportunities |

| Employers | Trained labour force, flexible labour force, flexible provision of training |
| Funding bodies | Value for money, reducing costs, higher student take-up |
| LEA contracts | Performance agreement based on price quality and student numbers |
| Training Education and Enterprise Directorate (TEED) | Quality-monitored-indicators, competitive, flexible, responsive to market, vocational orientation to be catalysts for industrial training |
| Training and enterprise councils | Partnership in planning and provision |
| Awarding bodies | Quality delivery, flexible offer, marketing, employer influence on course content, inputs and assessment |
| NCVQ | Competence-based assessment, work-based, access, no time constraint |
| Exam bodies | Money and numbers |
| Professional bodies | Standards and excellence – maintaining élitism |
| Staff | Job satisfaction, security, equal opportunities, staff development |
| Community | Life-long learning as investment in personal growth and development |

Although valuable for the reasons described, these expectations tend to describe the college in terms of what already exists. For this reason public statements are not very useful in creating a sense of mission amongst the staff or for changing the college's internal organisational culture.

*Mission statements*

A mission statement must clearly set out the purpose, values, behaviour and strategy which will guide the college forward. It is not actually necessary to write out a statement in order to carry it out, but this does help to communicate it to all staff.

Types of mission

1 Public mission statements: being public documents they can be shared with all those interested in the college and its future and therefore tend to be used for public relations activities rather than for planning purposes.
2 Private mission statements: these are intended to act as an internal planning tool and are therefore used internally to communicate and clarify purpose and strategy. This kind of mission statements is founded on the desire to create a consensus and clarity of purpose between management and staff. It acts as the starting point for decision-making by reminding all staff of the purpose, values, behaviour and general strategic direction of the college. Because such documents are not for circulation outside the college they can be used to encourage openness and to remove potential conflicts and disagreements. There is also space in private statements for sharing vision and hope for the future with staff.

Expressing the mission

There are many styles and models which could be used to describe a college's mission, but perhaps the most useful is the Ashridge Model. It's usefulness stems from the fact that it enables the dilemma of whether to be service-centred or business-centred to be addressed within one framework.

The model contains four elements: purpose, values, strategy and behaviour. It sees them as being linked together to reinforce each other in ways which provide a clear rationale for the college's behaviour and policies. The model is shown diagrammatically in Figure 6.1. In applying the model to a college it is as well to take each element in turn.

**Purpose** If it is to gain credibility there must be clarity of purpose demonstrated within the mission statement. It must also

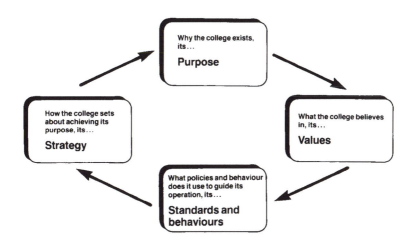

*Figure 6.1* The Ashridge Model for defining mission

be closely linked to the college's existing ethos and culture. In order to be clear about purpose the traditional questions must be asked:

- Who are our customers?
- What is the college for?
- For whose benefits are all the efforts being made?
- In addition to those who directly benefit, who are the other stakeholders, and what are their expectations of the college?

**Values**   The dilemma currently faced by colleges of whether they wish to be services and/or businesses can only be effectively worked through if they are clear about the values to be used as the framework for making operational judgements. These values will mean nothing unless they are clearly stated and communicated to staff through the behaviour of their managers. The value statement has three main purposes:

- to set out the framework of beliefs and moral principles which will underpin the college's culture
- to give meaning to the organisational norms and standards of behaviour practiced by the college
- to establish a rationale for behaviour which co-exists with and supports the college's operating strategy.

Within the Ashridge Model there are two useful rationales which link purpose and behaviour into one common strand of behaviour as exhibited by:

- the commercial rationale, which focused on strategy and the kinds of behaviour which will help the college to become financially successful
- the emotional, moral and ethical rationale, which focuses on values, and the treatment of people as individuals.

Both are important if colleges are to stick to their true educational mission of helping people to grow into autonomous, well-rounded individuals. An example of core values and philosophy statement for a college is shown below:

- Core values and philosophy: as we move into the future colleges will continue to experience rapid and discontinuous changes. It is vital that they are clear about the values which will guide their behaviour and actions. They are those which have shaped the college in the past and include:

  ♦ providing life-long learning opportunities, which are as accessible as possible and structured to allow individuals to pursue life, career and educational goals;
  ♦ encouraging all who wish to learn, irrespective of their age, ethnic background, physical disability, economic status, development stage or prior educational achievement, the only barriers being practical possibilities;
  ♦ giving support and leadership in the fields of education, training and economic development.

Individual achievement will continue to be the focus of the college's activities. The philosophy underpinning its services will therefore be based on:

- enabling individuals to meet their own specific needs in the fields of further and higher education/training related to academic and vocational education/training, access and transfer into higher education, and professional development at the beginning of their careers, to upgrade or develop new skills, or to engage in cultural enrichment or personal development;
- recognising that individuals have different learning styles, goals and life-circumstances and therefore require flexibility and choice between alternative ways of achieving their goals.

**Strategy** For the college to achieve its mission it must have a clear strategy. This will provide the logic behind planned actions and should address such issues as:

- Is it going to be community or commercially focused in its approach? If there is to be a balance between the two, what should that balance be?
- What markets is the college going to operate in, what position does it hold in these markets, and what competitive advantages does it intend to develop in the future?

**Behaviour** Unless converted into action through policy and behaviour guidelines, defining purpose, values and strategy will be paper exercises. These must be stated clearly enough to enable staff to make decisions which are in line with and support the overall direction of the college. It therefore follows that they must be clearly set out in the policy statements which in turn must be accompanied by well-understood implementation strategies aimed at ensuring that each policy is successful.

If the mission statement is to capture the emotional commitment and energy of the staff, policy and implementation strategies must convey the philosophical and moral rationale which underpin it and must in turn be acted out at all times by managers.

## Steps in developing a distinctive mission

Developing a distinct mission which is owned and acted out by the staff requires the college to:

- take time to get it right
- view the refinement of mission as a long-term project
- build up consensus on values, particularly in the top management team
- agree the model to be used for formulating the mission before beginning
- be clear about whose mission it is to be and who will write it
- have a clear strategy for communicating it internally to all staff
- fix review dates at regular intervals
- remember actions communicate better than words
- continually use the mission as a starting point for planning and decision-making

- formulate strategy and values together
- keep the mission alive as the guiding light for all the college's activities.

# Chapter 7

# Widening participation

## THE GROWING IMPORTANCE OF ENROLMENT MANAGEMENT

In considering its future development each college must work from the fact that the only real asset it has are its students. They generate the revenue it needs to continue operating and their success builds its reputation for excellence and its future viability as a successful college. In short, they are the only reason for its continuing existence. Widening participation will therefore be a key feature of tomorrow's colleges. It will involve the balancing of openness and accessibility against the pressures to maintain financial viability through a strong take-up rate across all programmes. This balancing act will be based on:

- enrolment planning for each part of the college's programmes and mode of study and attainment
- identifying potential students
- promoting the college's services
- dealing effectively with enquiries
- retention of students on programmes through effective support mechanisms
- ensuring successful student output.

Viability depends on all these factors, for it must be maintained through achieving a steady supply of students for all programmes, balanced by ensuring that all those wishing to attend the college have the advice and support needed to ensure their success.

## Enrolment planning

In order to plan take-up of all services those responsible must be able to assess potential demand and understand the factors which influence choice, linked to the factors which ensure their successful attendance and the achievement of desired outcomes. This requires adequate data on:

• the college's existing and potential client groups
• why individuals choose this particular college rather than another
• the characteristics of those who do and do not take up the college's services
• the positive and negative characteristics of the college's environment
• the characteristics of successful students
• the characteristics of those who drop out, or fail to complete their programmes
• the real benefits for each client group of attending colleges.

As in the past, good promotion, communications, marketing and public relations will continue to be important in supporting effective enrolment management.

## Identifying potential students

Meeting enrolment targets depends on the college's ability to match its programme to the needs of all its potential students. This requires information on the potential markets from which students may come. Such information would be collected by:

• mapping the potential demand for each of the college's existing services against the needs of the geographical area which it serves;
• breaking down potential demand into market segments based on the specific characteristics and needs of each segment;
• identifying the college's current performance by matching actual demand against potential demand for each market segment, thereby establishing areas of good and poor performance, and identifying gaps in the market;
• monitoring to assess possible changes in existing demand patterns;

- measuring student satisfaction and perceptions of the college with special attention focused on barriers to access and problems with maintaining attendance;
- monitoring the student population in terms of the groups who currently participate, and matching these against non-participants, identifying the characteristics of each group and reasons for participation and non-participation.

*Community needs audits*

In addition to using this kind of traditional marketing analysis, some colleges are also developing audits of local community needs as part of their assessment of potential markets.

The framework for conducting such an audit will depend on the complexity of the environment and the degree of detail being sought. A basic framework could comprise:

- Community profile, used to provide a picture of the population being served by the college in terms of:

  ♦ age mix
  ♦ gender profile
  ♦ ethnic mix
  ♦ community issues
  ♦ employment profile
  ♦ unpaid work profile
  ♦ needs of the non-waged

- Education/training needs profile, used to develop a picture of the education/training needs of specific employers and the community generally in terms of:

  ♦ employment education/training needs
  ♦ changing employment patterns
  ♦ re-training needs
  ♦ accreditation opportunities
  ♦ work-based learning needs
  ♦ need for assessment services
  ♦ community education/training needs
  ♦ requirements for supporting community services
  ♦ requirements for supporting community development

- Help and guidance networks, used to establish the availability of help and guidance within the community in terms of:

- ◆ the kinds of help and guidance available
- ◆ gaps in the help and guidance provided
- ◆ levels of demand, particularly in areas of help and guidance which the college can support
- ◆ the need to establish links into the college's services
- ◆ information requirements on the college's services

- Community awareness assessment: In order to balance all the other forms of analysis the college needs to conduct an assessment of the level of awareness across the whole community of the services it offers and the effectiveness of its promotional activities.

Maintaining viability as a college depends upon developing an understanding of the potential level of demand for all services, and knowing why potential students attend. This requires:

- a strategy for optimising the take-up of all the college's services;
- a market research group with responsibility for carrying out the market analysis and building community profiles;
- a marketing plan broken down into market segments based on knowledge of each segment and sensitivity to changes in economic and non-economic activity;
- understanding of the groups who do not take up college services and what they perceive to be the barriers to access and participation;
- understanding of the participating students' perception of college;
- understanding of the fit between student needs and college provision, along with those items in the college's programme or built environment which can be altered to achieve greater success;
- knowledge of the effectiveness of the college's promotional activities;
- understanding of the effect of fee levels on demand and potential elasticity in relationship to costs;
- understanding of the effects of fee levels on equal opportunities and potential effects of alternative fee-waiving strategies.

*Setting enrolment targets*

Targets must be based on an assessment of potential demands and the availability of resources. Factors to be taken into account when setting targets include:

- Demographic trends: possibly the most important non-market stimulus to potential demand as they represent the numbers and categories of potential students.
- Take-up rates: to be considered alongside reasons for non-participation and opportunities for removing barriers at the time of setting targets.
- Changes in the labour market: most labour market data drags behind the market and cannot be relied upon. However, it can provide useful pointers in the form of generalisations to be validated against the specific situation in which the college finds itself.
- Unmet demand: to be assessed through market studies, which are particularly important when opening up new markets such as the accreditation of prior learning, assessment of work-based learning and assessment on demand, which will require piloting and supporting past their financial break-even points.
- Economic forecasts: to be used with caution in an attempt to predict down- or up-swings in the level of economic activity. They are then used to assess how changes might affect demand for college places, or for qualified students. They can also be used to assess demand for update-training for those already in employment along with the need for accreditation and assessment services.
- Elasticity of demand: similar to take-up rate in as much as it measures the responsiveness to changes in the take-up of college services in relation to market segment and changes in the level of economic activity.
- Cross elasticity: based on an assessment of the likelihood that a potential student will substitute one college or programme within a college for another as the price varies between the two. Thus, although the demand for further education and training may remain relatively inelastic, the cross-elasticity may vary. This helps to explain variations in demand between different colleges for similar programmes.
- Economic benefits: the direct economic benefits which students feels will accrue to them as a result of attending college and enhancing their qualifications.

- Other benefits: all the non-economic benefits which students feel they will gain from college attendance, i.e. personal growth, improved opportunities for sport, social activities, etc.
- Direct costs: the real amount of all costs the student will be expected to bear as a result of attending college, including fees, books, travel, etc.
- Opportunity costs: the potential income lost to the student through not working full-time, taking time off, or through lost overtime, in order to attend college.
- Rate of return: in terms of differential between qualified and non-qualified individuals in the situation where they intend to use their qualifications.
- The raising of recruitment thresholds: students are aware of the tendency of employers to raise threshold qualifications when recruiting. Qualifications may therefore become screening devices, and the job may not require the skills achieved whilst obtaining them.

Some of the factors described above exert considerably more influence than others and colleges will need to consider the impact of each within their own situations. Some form of rating scale should be used alongside each of the factors, matched alongside each programme area. The most important factors appear to be:

1 Prices, fees and all financial considerations. The discretionary fee-waiving policy can have an important impact on demand.
2 Demographic factors/employment selection: both have a considerable impact in determining the levels of aggregate demand for places across all college programmes.
3 Ethos and reputation, which are major factors in influencing demand.

Aggregate demand is relatively unresponsive to:

(a) increases and decreases in labour market activity, although there will be movement between part- and full-time within the total;
(b) the demand for qualifications from employers;
(c) the rate of return as assessed by each individual student.

# Chapter 8

# Attracting potential students

## PROMOTING THE COLLEGE'S SERVICES

Promotional activities are central to the process of making potential students aware of the full range of opportunities available. There is often a difference between what the college thinks potential students know about it and what they actually know. The gap this creates needs to be closed if the college is to satisfy its role in the community.

In order to ensure that all potential students know what services are available, the college's promotional activities must:

- give positive messages in ways which capture the interest of potential students;
- be seen by all prospective students;
- indicate clearly the full range of opportunities available;
- convey the range of services in a style and language understandable by potential students;
- convey to potential students that it is worth taking up the services on offer.

In order to achieve these aims, care must be taken with the content, design and style of promotional materials, along with the image of the college which they convey.

### Building a promotional network

To get its message across to all segments of the market it wishes to serve the college will need to develop a network which targets each specific segment. To be effective, this may mean that a different promotional approach is needed for each. Such a network can be built up and maintained by selecting appropriate methods from the following:

- Targeting all promotional materials specifically to the needs of the potential students being approached.
- Building up direct contacts through personal approaches followed by visits to workplaces, community groups, etc.
- Using targeted mailing lists for each of the potential market segments.
- Capitalising on display opportunities such as careers conventions, public exhibitions, conferences, etc.
- Establishing focal points such as college festivals built around open days, and displays of work, which aim to show potential students the range of services on offer and what kind of establishment the college is.

*Factors influencing student choice*

The main reasons which motivate students to choose one college rather than another can be grouped under four broad headings:

1  programme choice and the openness and accessibility of the programmes on offer;
2  characteristics of the college;
3  characteristics of students;
4  perceived level of student support.

The college's ability to manage its enrolment across the variety of programmes and alternative modes of attendance is closely tied to its level of understanding of the ways in which the above four points affect students in their choice of a college.

The range of opportunities available

The first and major influence on students' choice of a college is the closeness of the programmes on offer to their own perceived needs and ambitions. This is closely followed by the ease with which they feel they could take up the programme and their judgement about their likelihood of success.

From the individual student's point of view the programme issues centre around the following questions:

- Is the specific programme or combination of programmes I want to study available?
- Does it (or do they) appear to meet my personal needs?
- Does it offer the right subjects or combination of subjects?
- Does the power appear to lie:

  ◆ with the college, because it offers rigid programme structures into which the student must fit?
  ◆ with the students, who have an element of choice and ability to structure the programme to their specific needs?

- Do the programmes on offer enable me to:

  ◆ choose a learning style to meet my needs, i.e. taught or part self-directed study?
  ◆ choose from a range of modules to meet my own specific needs?
  ◆ get value for what I have already learned from the accreditation of my prior learning?
  ◆ choose whether to build up credit and carry it forward?
  ◆ choose the method of assessment to enable me to succeed?

- If I make the wrong choice will I be able to change programme easily?
- Does the programme have external credibility, and will it be accepted by other institutions?
- Will I be able to use the outcome of my study to progress on to the next stage of my development?

The characteristics of the college

In making their selection students will be influenced by the unique characteristics of each of the colleges available to them. In attempting to win students, colleges must try to understand the characteristics of their organisation which influence student choice and which of these they can alter in order to increase student participation levels.

All the characteristics of a college are, of course, changeable in the longer term, but for a realistic assessment it is as well to concentrate on the things which can be changed or made more effective in the short term. A rolling programme can be devised to tackle the major, longer-term issues.

Taking the short-term perspective, the characteristics influencing student choice can be divided into fixed and variable categories. Fixed characteristics include:

- Location: this may prevent some students attending, but it is difficult to change the location of a college. Outreach arrangements can be considered where appropriate to widen participation for some groups.
- Internal environment: the internal environment of the college, its state of repair and decoration, can have a major impact on student choice. Layout and student space such as refectories, common rooms, private study areas and library facilities all have an impact.
- Staff structure: staff profile in terms of age, gender, ethics, length of service and skills are all relatively fixed in the short term. Attitudes towards the kind of staff they would prefer to work with can have a major impact on student choice.
- Aggregate funds available: although not directly assessed by students the funds available to the college influence its ability to maintain and improve its environment and the other factors influencing student choice.

Variable characteristics can be changed by the college in the short term and are therefore a major factor to be considered when planning enrolment. They include:

- Programmes on offer: the structure and style of programmes will have a major effect on student choice. Modular and credit accumulation opportunities are of great interest to students as is the ability to change programmes within the same initiation.
- Modes of attendance/methods of obtaining accreditation: flexibility in these areas are important to students, particularly when they provide more openness and accessibility.
- Fee policies: direct out-of-pocket expenses are of critical importance to most students. College policies in this area, along with the fee-waiving policy, have a direct impact on student choice.
- Student support programmes: the range, type and amount of support which students feel they will receive from the college are also taken into account.
- College policies and treatment of students: the way students perceive the college policies and their application to students will have an impact on their choice.

Both fixed and variable factors need to be assessed when setting targets and worked on in order to increase participation. Colleges need to assess their own ability to change in order to become more attractive to prospective students. Setting characteristics out into a table for analysis is perhaps the best approach, and this is done in Table 8.1. Each characteristic should be graded according to the college's judgement of its ability to change it and make it more attractive to students.

*Table 8.1* Fixed and variable characteristics of colleges

| Fixed characteristics | Variable characteristics |
| --- | --- |
| Location | Programme structure |
| Internal environment | Modes of attendance |
| Staff structure | Methods of achieving accreditation |
| Aggregate funds available | Fee policies |
|  | Student support programmes |
|  | Policies and treatment of students |

Student characteristics

Among the factors which influence students' decisions to enrol for a particular college programme is their individual background, which includes such things as their parents' education and financial and socio-economic factors, all of which seem to correlate closely with students' decisions to continue studying. Added to these factors are students' previous and existing patterns of educational success, their cultural backgrounds and gender, all of which also appear to be important influences. These characteristics can be grouped together to indicate the full range of potential influences, as shown in Figure 8.1.

These characteristics described in Figure 8.1 combine in unique ways for each individual and the weight which each exerts on the potential student will also vary with their individual circumstances. However, they are not the only elements influencing choice; they combine with the programme and the institutional characteristics described on pp. 74–7 and together they all influence the final decision made by the student.

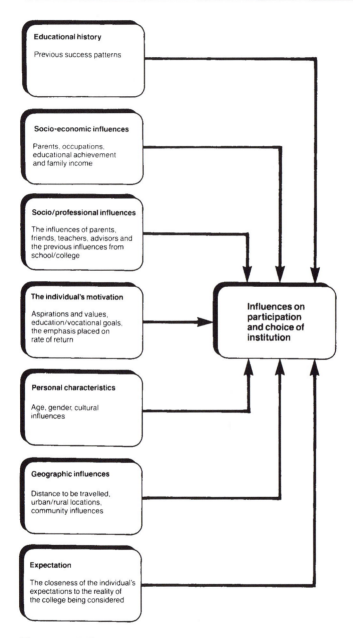

*Figure 8.1* Influences on participation and choice of college

Student/college compatibility

Concentrating on retaining students after their enrolment onto programmes is just as important as the efforts made in attracting them to the college in the first place. There needs to be a close match between their goals and interests and the ability of the environmental, academic and social characteristics of the college to meet their expectations.

To be successful the college must attempt to match the expectations of potential students with what it can realistically provide. If a close match can be achieved it will increase the motivation and performance of students and raise the retention rate.

In attempting to achieve a good fit between students and the college, it is important to realise that:

- if students enrol at college with unrealistic expectations about the programme they are likely to have problems in remaining on it;
- it therefore follows that students who enter programmes with realistic expectations are the ones most likely to succeed;
- when a fit exists between the needs and perceptions of students and the characteristics of the college the aims of both are more likely to be achieved;
- colleges which focus on how it feels from the students point of view are the ones most likely to succeed.

Searching out answers to the above and structuring the information and guidance given to students to ensure that their expectations are realistic is a crucial element in student retention and success.

## DEALING EFFECTIVELY WITH ENQUIRIES

If the college is to convert as many enquiries as possible into enrolments, it needs a standard procedure for maintaining contact with prospective students as they progress through the enquiry, advice, application and admission stages.

Every enquiry should be given the status of prospective student and in some way recorded to enable follow-up to take place. A computerised database will be the best vehicle for this. Each college will need to develop its own model for dealing most effectively with the enquiry, advice, application and admission processes. It also has to be accepted that not all student needs can be met by a standard model, and flexibility will be needed to provide sufficient scope to accommodate all needs and to improve the efficiency of student care. If all the aims of student care programmes are to be met, the system will need to include advice and guidance to ensure that individuals are not following inappropriate routes to achievement.

In the move towards a learner-centred college it will be necessary to identify incremental objectives on the path towards a fully flexible college. The basis of this move must be an enquiry, advice, application and admissions system which accommodates the delivery of a modularised curriculum, roll on/roll off provision, individualised learning programmes, accreditation of prior learning and credit accumulation. All these developments will inevitably lead to the distinctions between full- and part-time students becoming blurred if not entirely removed.

The objectives of the full procedure and, more specifically, the objectives of each stage of the procedure, must be designed to ensure that it achieves the overall objective of ensuring a higher level of satisfaction for each and every student. In designing the system it is therefore important that each and every stage of the process is compatible with all others so that total cohesion and integration is achieved. The process is illustrated in Figure 8.2.

It may not be possible to deal with all enquiries through one admissions point. One way of integrating multiple locations is through a computer network. The networking of any admissions system will need to incorporate all enquiry/admission points across the college, all of which must also be linked into the college's student records system.

Consideration must also be given to the amount of time needed to log data into the system and any queries which may result from this. This analysis must be based on an examination of the ratios of how the college receives its enquiries, i.e. by telephone, personal callers, written requests. This kind of analysis will indicate the 'real time' problems of logging enquiries, along with the staffing ratio and number of computer terminals needed. Analysis should also be made of the pattern of enquiries so that issues of peak demand, queuing and waiting time can be adequately addressed. The diagram in Figure 8.3 indicates a typical demand pattern.

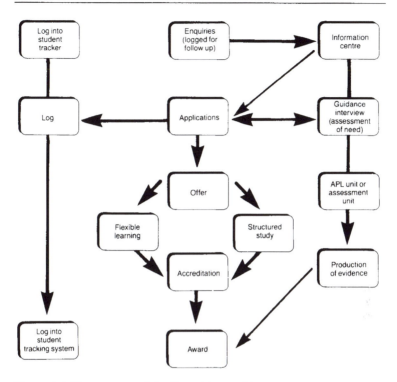

*Figure 8.2* The process of dealing with enquiries
*Source*: Based on the work of Steven Holt at Croydon College

The work content involved in handling the enquiries will also need assessing. If the staff are required to give brief advice and hand out promotional leaflets, this will take considerably less time than logging enquiries and asking for personal details for data entry.

The use of a logging system will inevitably lead to a change in the approach towards dealing with enquiries from potential students, based on the following factors:

- Developing a database constructed to provide detailed information on:

   ♦ number of enquiries
   ♦ method of enquiry, i.e. personal callers, telephone, written requests

**Applications received: September – July**

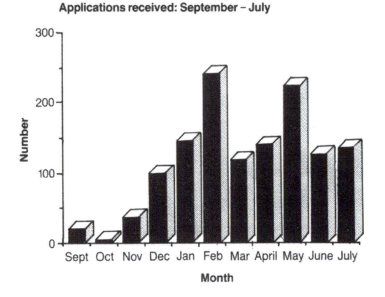

*Figure 8.3* Applications profile

- ◆ nature of the enquiry, i.e. by subject qualifications or mode of attendance, for accreditation of prior learning or assessment, etc.
- ◆ information issued, i.e. by prospectus, specialist leaflet
- ◆ enquiries for services not offered by the college
- ◆ search by name of other personal details
- ◆ search by enquiry number
- ◆ search and report by status of record
- ◆ aggregate reports of all the above
- • Working on the concept of student tracking, so that it is possible to target enquirers who have not returned an application form, to issue follow-up letters or invite them to an open evening.
- • Having educated guidance or planning built into the system and offered as a free follow-up service to those who have not followed their enquiry with an application.

The specification for handling enquiries should be designed:

- • to ensure that it is based on a standard cover sheet which mirrors the enrolment form. This will save time later and help with the transfer of data into the student records system;

- with an application form (which for the reasons outlined above also mirrors the enrolment form) to be given to each enquirer;
- to allocate by computer a number to each enquiry, which later becomes the student number, and which will be required on the application form by the member of staff handling the enquiry. Alternatively, all application forms could be pre-printed with numbers, which could be entered into the computer at the time of enquiry;
- to establish an enquiry record which is networked and accessible to all those administering admissions;
- to ensure that on receipt of the application form the number is called up and the relevant details from the enquiry upgraded to application status. The upgrading should only be accessible to those dealing with admissions but reports should have wider circulation.

# Chapter 9

# Enabling students to succeed

## RETENTION OF STUDENTS

Attracting students to college without giving them satisfying life-long learning is expensive. Student retention, with its focus on providing a good service which builds loyalty and individual satisfaction and links the student to the college, must therefore be an important element in the design of services.

Keeping students depends upon:

- understanding their perceptions of the service they require and then concentrating on providing it
- considering each student to be a life-long learner who will tell many others what they think about the college
- paying careful attention to both the fixed and the variable characteristics of the college
- being supportive of requests from students
- saying 'yes' as often as possible
- working on appearances; buildings, staff, service areas
- developing information and guidance facilities
- retention being part of the marketing approach
- asking students what they think
- making sure that everything the college offers is of top quality
- developing a strong programme identity
- making good first impressions
- developing a close relationship with students
- obtaining as much information about potential and actual students as possible
- offering an attractive programme
- looking for ways to stretch students

- tracking what is effective with students
- handling each student as effectively and professionally as possible
- viewing student complaints as opportunities to do better
- making it as easy as possible for students to obtain the services and support they need
- promising only what can be delivered.

Adapted from: La Neta L Carlock, LERN Conference, 1989

### Guidance and support services

The flexibility in tomorrow's colleges will need to be based upon effective student support. Colleges will therefore need to have high profiles and highly effective student services, as shown in Figure 9.1.

As participation is widened to include non-traditional groups of students, guidance and support services will play a much more essential role in enabling their success, because the variety of learning and accreditation services available to students will cause confusion. Making sense of the opportunities will be difficult and individuals will need personalised help to enable them to do so. As the patterns of educational and training opportunities grow, the importance of guidance and support frameworks will therefore increase.

*Types of guidance and support*

The types of guidance and support needed in the future are already becoming clearly established. They will be further developed in the future and offered to students in a more coherent and integrated way. These services will be based on:

- personal guidance frameworks, to help students with personal problems, including personal barriers to study, financial aid, accommodation and child care;
- education/training guidance frameworks, which will help individuals plan their pathways towards personal education/ training goals. The focus will very much be on access, progression, and the attainment of personal goals;
- career/vocational guidance frameworks, which will help individuals plan for career growth and decide on the path to be followed if success is to be achieved.

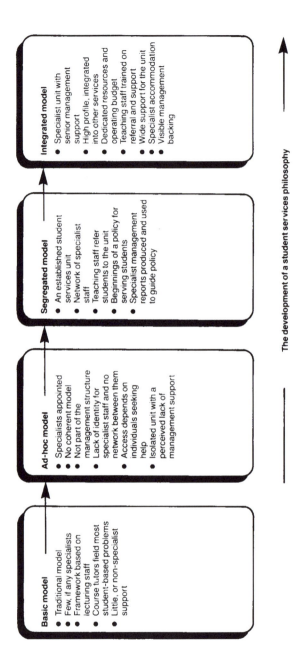

**Basic model**

- Traditional model
- Few, if any specialists
- Framework based on lecturing staff
- Course tutors field most student-based problems
- Little, or non-specialist support

**Ad-hoc model**

- Specialists appointed
- No coherent model
- Not part of the management structure
- Lack of identity for specialist staff and no network between them
- Access depends on individuals seeking help
- Isolated unit with a perceived lack of management support

**Segregated model**

- An established student services unit
- Network of specialist staff
- Teaching staff refer students to the unit
- Beginnings of a policy for serving students
- Specialist management reports produced and used to guide policy

**Integrated model**

- Specialist unit with senior management support
- High profile, integrated into other services
- Dedicated resources and operating budget
- Teaching staff trained on referral and support
- Wide support for the unit
- Specialist accommodation
- Visible management backing

The development of a student services philosophy

*Figure 9.1* The development of student services

Although most colleges already offer these services, their importance will grow in the future in order to provide an essential firm framework of support around the flexibility offered by modularisation and flexible learning. The guiding principals will be:

- a focus on the needs of individuals
- confidentiality and personal support
- impartial non-directive advice
- availability and accessibility
- publicity.

*The future role of guidance and support*

The future role will be similar to that of today with one essential difference: the growing importance of feed-back into the college's planning and quality improvement processes. The services will therefore have two primary objectives:

1 Helping potential students to make effective choices based on knowledge and understanding of the range of opportunities available to them, and offering effective support to enable them to overcome any difficulties.
2 Enabling the college to improve the range and quality of its support service through feedback on such items as:

   (a) barriers to access and progression and how they might be removed
   (b) the match between programmes on offer and actual student needs
   (c) improvements in guidance and support services.

The pursuit of these two objectives will translate into benefits both for students and for the college.

Benefits to potential students

Although potential students may be aware of their own perceived education/training needs, they may be unclear about the opportunities available to them, or the ways in which they might go about satisfying their needs.

Effective guidance and support services will help them to move their lives forward by:

- helping them to clarify their personal goals
- informing them of the range of possibilities open to them
- identifying their specific requirements and helping them to devise action plans to meet them
- helping them to obtain credit for their past education/training
- clarifying the support available to them during the learning and accreditation process.

Benefits to the college

As competition increases for students, highly effective student guidance and support services will demonstrate the college's commitment towards openness, flexibility of response and equal opportunities. If the services are set up with effective feed-back loops into the college's planning processes they can provide information on how to remove barriers to access and improve the match between the programmes on offer and student needs. The future effectiveness of the college will therefore be improved if the guidance and support services focus on:

- developing an understanding in the college of the public's perceptions of its services, and the knowledge gap between what it has to offer and what the public thinks it offers;
- identifying the real barriers to taking up and participating in the college's services;
- reducing non-completions by ensuring that potential students have the best possible information on which to base their decisions to take up the college's services;
- providing information and support services which focus on the specific needs of each of the college's client groups;
- providing feedback into the college's planning and implementation processes which improves the monitoring quality of the services on offer and makes them more appropriate to student needs.

## THE FRAMEWORK OF GUIDANCE AND SUPPORT

As a sound guidance and support framework becomes increasingly important to the college's future success, a fully integrated system of on-going support of the kind illustrated in Figure 9.2 will be needed.

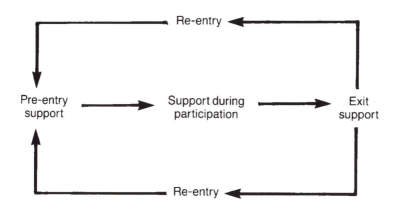

*Figure 9.2* The framework of guidance and support

**Pre-entry support**

As colleges become ever more active in developing structures to support life-long learning, the role of pre-entry support will become even more important, in order to encourage a wider section of the population into learning.

Enquiries at this pre-entry stage will need to be dealt with sensitively if potential students are to be encouraged to follow up their enquiry with positive action. Those who have had negative experiences with education may feel alienated and intimidated by the thought of having to approach an educational institution again.

At its most basic, pre-entry guidance and support will be concerned with giving accurate information in a friendly, non-threatening manner. At this point, the prospective student will not be fully aware of:

- the learning/accreditation opportunities open to them
- how to identify the route to learning/accreditation which is most accessible to them and which best suits their needs
- the reception they are going to get from the college or its response to their needs.

Guidance and support at this stage will therefore fall into two broad categories, as follows:

*Information/guidance*

- All the learning and accreditation opportunities open to them
- All the ways of taking up the opportunities, modes of attendance, flexible learning, accreditation of prior learning, assessment on demand, etc.
- The services available for assessment in or out of the workplace, accreditation of non-traditional learning, portfolio preparation, etc.
- Alternative places to study

*Support*

- The personal counselling and guidance services available
- Advice on action planning
- Financial aid services
- Educational advice and guidance to ensure that the action plan is appropriate and coherent with the individual's desired outcome
- Careers and progression advice

Both guidance and support services need to be integrated because it is clear that neither on its own is enough. Students will need help in clarifying their needs, linking them to the right programme and assessing the credit they can obtain from previous study, all of which need the help of an experienced practitioner.

### Support during participation

Once they have decided to take part in one of the college's activities, new students will require access and guidance services such as:

- diagnostic testing
- support into learning
- learning styles assessment
- accreditation of prior learning
- portfolio building and presentation
- induction programmes to support literacy, numeracy and communication skills.

In addition to entry support, learners will require personal guidance and support throughout their learning or accreditation programmes. This will become increasingly more important as modularisation of programmes and flexible learning and credit accumulation opportunities become progressively more available. Such support can be arranged under two broad headings, as shown below. The distinction between these different support needs is reflected in the staffing of advice and support centres.

| *Personal support* | *Learning support* |
|---|---|
| • Personal counselling | • Access to a personal tutor to provide feedback on progress |
| • Academic tutor support | • Help with study skills |
| • Adequate social and private study facilities | • Basic skills support, such as language skills |
| • Peer group support such as women's only groups | • Support for students with physical disabilities |
| • Child care facilities | • Access to flexible learning workshops which enable students to make progress at their own pace |
| | • Assessment services |
| | • Advice on progress being made, including summarative records and credit accumulation |

## Support at the point of leaving the college

As we move more towards the notion of life-long learning and the need for individuals to return later to continue their studies, exit support becomes much more important. The range of services provided should include:

• enabling students to take advantage of their achievements
• guidance on the learners' next steps
• progression to further study

- careers advice and guidance
- preparation for employment
- information on linking back into the college's programmes should the need arise in the future
- information on making contact with other networks.

By providing an integrated system of on-going guidance and support, colleges will be more able to:

- maintain a high level of participation across the full range of their services
- improve retention and success rates
- increase satisfaction and build a lasting relationship with students
- improve links with individuals, employers and the wider community
- enhance their image and reputation.

*Effectiveness of information and guidance services*

To improve the effectiveness of their information and guidance services colleges will need to:

- develop close linkages between these services and the academic staff
- establish an effective information and guidance support network both inside the college and with other agencies
- provide a good operating environment for the services at a prominent central location within the college
- provide an adequate number of properly trained advisors and support staff
- establish a monitoring and control system for the services based on clear performance indicators
- ensure the services feed back into the college's planning and decision-making structure so that they are continually improved and matched to changing student needs.

# Chapter 10

# Organisational factors affecting flexibility

College organisations have for some time been coping with the conflicting problems of attempting to provide some stability for staff whilst at the same time responding to pressures to bring about change. These pressures are likely to be sharpened up as colleges move into the future.

Leaving aside the arguments of appropriate structures which dominated the 1970s and 1980s, it is now clear that there is no single best way of organising and that colleges should move their focus away from structure towards functional requirements for success.

## FUNCTIONAL REQUIREMENTS

It is now accepted that educational organisations are dynamic in the sense that each part affects the functions of every other part in some way. At the centre of the college's organisation must be the focus of learning and achievement which is supported by the rest of the system. The functional requirements of an educational organisation are, therefore, that both learning and achievement take place to the advantage of students. The inter-relationship between the different parts is shown in Figure 10.1.

Given this model of inter-relatedness any development of a college's organisation must recognise the need to link all aspects of the model together, and at the same time to see them as part of the wider system. Such a view is the basis of curriculum-led staff development and leads into the notions of curriculum-led organisational and resource development.

This understanding of the inter-related nature of college organisations is particularly important when introducing new ideas such as the accreditation of prior learning.

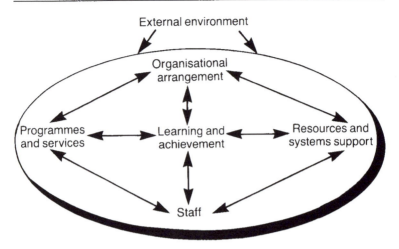

*Figure 10.1* The inter-relationship of colleges as organisations

An integrated approach, based on the analysis of functional requirements, leads to the concept of core objectives to be met by college organisations, which will mean that the colleges must be able to:

1  Meet its corporate objectives, by ensuring that

(a) each part of the organisation functionally reflects these objectives and clearly indicates accountability for their delivery;

(b) colleges facing change must deal effectively with any existing power structures which prevent this match between functional performance and objective achievement from taking place.

2  Learn and adapt to changing needs, by responding quickly and effectively to maintain a close match between its services and customer needs. Adaptability must be linked to the idea of organisational learning, based on recognition that maintaining a lasting competitive edge rests on becoming a learning organisation. This is based on two linked ideas:

(a) learning how to solve the immediate problem facing the organisation; and

(b) learning from the process and storing this learning for future use.

This kind of learning increases the ability of the organisation, enables it to grow in confidence, empowers it to undertake future learning, and will be the key to survival and development for colleges in the future.

3  Maintain a feeling of internal calm, which will only be achieved if staff have confidence in their managers and the systems which are intended to help them in coping with change. Most changes now require cross-college responses which cut across existing systems of management and control and therefore threaten the internal calm. The notion of organisational climate, dealt with on pp. 96–8 is a major factor in providing stability and calm even in situations of rapid change.

These three requirements are difficult to obtain and rely on a clear functional analysis of requirements linked to the idea of developing systems which support change and enable the college to build a learning organisation.

In the short term colleges are having to structure their organisational arrangements to:

- find the best functional arrangement to meet the current needs of their customers and staff;
- achieve the best possible match between teaching and learning, monitoring and control systems, specialist services and the configuration of all support services;
- ensure that their information and control systems are adequate for all the tasks which need to be performed effectively to ensure the delivery of the college's core mission;
- achieve the best trade off between teaching and social and formal organisational needs, and between the cost of co-ordination and the benefits of specialisation.

In the long term colleges will have to structure their organisations:

- to be capable of adapting appropriately to changing needs and be capable of integrating new requirements into their delivery and support systems.

The future health of college organisation depends on bringing these short- and long-term aims together. This means focusing the management of the college onto a time frame, constructed around three different time horizons:

1 Day-to-day performance (short-term time horizon), which measures this performance in terms of efficiency and effectiveness in the use of all resources.

2 Annual performance (medium-term time horizon): during each annual cycle new programmes and services will be introduced and others changed to meet new customer needs. This annual co-alignment, often within existing resources, is critical to the college's longer-term success.

3 Three/five year strategic planning (long-term time horizon): the college's longer-term health will depend on it regularly addressing within its strategic planning:

(a) its ability to predict and plan its response to shifts in changing customer needs;

(b) its ability to develop staff and systems to cope with the above changes.

The long-term health of the college depends on the capacity of its management to maintain a balance between all three time horizons at once. Undue emphasis on any one of them at the expense of the others will be unhealthy in the long term. Equally important, however, is the development of an internal climate which is supportive and responsive to change.

## ORGANISATIONAL CLIMATE

If the college's organisation is to respond effectively to the kinds of changes put forward in this book, then it must have the kind of internal organisational climate which allows change to take place.

In essence a college's internal organisational climate is based on the perceptions and feelings of its members, who perceive it as being either supportive or non-supportive to the role they are expected to perform.

A college's internal climate has the following characteristics:

• an element of reality which enables staff to agree and be able to share their experiences of it;
• a shared perception which distinguishes it from such individual experiences as level of personal motivation;
• although not unchanging, it has an air of continuity;
• it impacts on the behaviour of individual members of staff as they undertake their tasks.

An effective climate would be one which encouraged risk-taking and change within a framework of individual achievement. Climates are often set by the organisation's leader, who has a major impact on how the climate develops. In general terms it results from the interaction of two sets of conditions:

1 how the college operates formally through its organisational structure and treatment of staff, along with all other management practices and procedures;
2 how the college's informal structure operates through the interaction of its staff.

Climate is therefore an expression of the prevailing ethos within which managers make decisions, along with how the staff operate and feel about their work. The right kind of climate is essential to the introduction of new ideas such as the accreditation of prior learning.

### Determinants of organisational climate

Given its variability it is difficult to be precise about the exact nature of an organisation's climate and what determines its shape or feel. Despite this difficulty the following factors appear to be important in shaping climate:

- Organisational clarity: does the college have clear and accepted goals, expressed in the form of published plans, aims and measurable objectives, expressed in ways which give the college a clear sense of direction?
- Decision-making structure: is this clear and supported by appropriate information being created and made available to decision-makers?
- Monitoring and control systems: are these systems capable of reviewing progress towards the college's objectives?
- Organisational effectiveness: do all parts know their own and their shared objectives with other parts of the organisation? Are they able to integrate their activities and communicate effectively?
- Performance: are all staff aware of the emphasis placed on accountability for results, in terms of the college's aims and objectives?
- Management style: this is an important aspect of the management of change. Does it:

- ◆ enable members of staff to feel encouraged and supported in their work?
- ◆ make the pattern of delegated authority clear in terms of each member of staff's perceptions of their freedom of action?

- Responsiveness: the extent to which the staff see the college as being dynamic and responsive to change.
- Compensation: based on staff judgements or perceptions of the rewards available and their fair distribution in relation to effort.
- Staff development: the degree to which staff feel they have opportunities to develop their true potential within the college.

These factors combine to create a climate which is either supportive or non-supportive to the changes needed to make a flexible and responsive college.

# Chapter 11

# Managing change: assessing the amount of change required

## THE CHANGING NATURE OF CHANGE

As discussed earlier (see p. 12) colleges have always responded to change. The difference now is that the amount of change they are having to face is increasing and the amount of time required to respond to it is getting shorter. The pace and direction of change will mean that over the next ten years colleges will become very different places from what they are today.

In the past, continuous predictable change has been the dominant force and colleges have grown used to managing well. However, they are now increasingly being asked to respond to unpredictable or discontinuous changes, which they are finding more difficult. The differences between the two types of change are shown below:

- Continuous or predictable change is based on an extension of the past, so the skills and knowledge it requires are already available and planning for its implementation is easier.
- Discontinuous or unpredictable change is not based on an extension of the past and therefore requires novel responses which are not based on established skills and knowledge. The time frame for introducing unpredictable change is often much shorter, which makes it a more uncomfortable form of change to face up to.

The ratio between the types of change is in itself changing from one where predictable change was the largest component to one where unpredictable change is becoming the more dominant force. This changing ratio makes it much more difficult for college managers as both the complexity and the time needed to manage change increases.

## MANAGING THE PRESSURES TO CHANGE

An important aspect for colleges introducing change is an awareness of the forces which the proposed change will generate, and the possible sources of resistance which might arise, so that contingency plans can be drawn up to resist or harness them.

Resistance to change needs to be put into context because by its nature change nearly always has to face barriers. These need to be assessed carefully as some of them might act as indicators that there are basic problems inherent in the change itself, or the way in which it is being introduced.

The perceived need to change is often based on the notion that there is a gap between the current situation and what ought to be. Performance gaps are the main force for change in education particularly in the areas of creating more openness and flexibility, along with the introduction of new services such as the accreditation of prior learning. Resistance to these changes stems from the cultural, social and psychological forces within the college's organisation.

Taking the argument further, it would appear that those who are in the position of being able to bring about change must be able either to open up new performance gaps or to capitalise on existing openings in order to use them as levers to bring about change. They must also have the influence or power necessary to provide both the direction and the necessary means to close the gap.

Having perceived a performance gap there are two options available:

1 To raise performance by initiating the actions needed to close the gap, i.e. devising plans to make the college more open and flexible by taking on the resistance to the introduction of new activities such as assessment on demand and the accreditation of prior learning.
2 To lower expectations of the desired level of performance expected, i.e. by dismissing new services as not being appropriate to the college, or on the grounds of low demand for them.

Whilst the second option may, on occasions, become a pragmatic necessity only the first one will bring about an actual change in the college's performance.

One of the major factors to guard against in implementing change is that of unrealistic expectations of the speed with which the proposed change will bring about improvement. This is particularly important as the disappointment caused by unrealistic expectations often causes resistance to change in the future. It is therefore particularly important not to overestimate the pay off of any proposed change.

If the outcome is lower than predicted then it will be necessary to take steps to adjust expectations downwards or adjust performance upwards.

Adjusting expectations downwards can be achieved by:

- showing that the initial expectations resulted from claims which could not easily be satisfied
- pointing out that uncontrollable circumstances are preventing the change from achieving its full potential
- Demonstrating that other users are experiencing even poorer results.

Adjusting performance upwards can be achieved by:

- using staff development and training activities to underpin and support the proposed change
- contact and interaction with other colleges undertaking the same changes
- having a strong contingent of staff with wide experience and positive outlook towards the college and keeping its services up to date
- putting energy into pushing the proposed change through the inertia which it will inevitably face in its opening stages
- developing a 'critical mass' of staff who support the proposed change and who will put their energy behind its success.

### The motivation to introduce change

In addition to the changing needs of potential clients, there are other reasons why colleges may introduce new services. These may be grouped under the following general headings:

- Educational leadership: to become an educational leader in a particular field such as flexible learning or assessment on demand.

- Improvements in efficiency: to improve the efficiency of the college's systems, which leads to greater flexibility and responsiveness.
- Relevance: to introduce new equipment and systems which ensure that the curriculum and services offered are more relevant to the needs of learners.
- Responsiveness: to increase responsiveness to the needs of customers, e.g. through the introduction of new services such as the accreditation of prior learning.
- Professionalism: this includes many of the above under the general heading of trying to do the best possible for clients within existing resources.

Often these elements combine with the need to improve the curriculum or to offer new services as the motivation or driving force behind the pressures for change. The major question remains: 'Does this change actually need to be carried out, or is it being done for other reasons such as following fashion?' Change often releases negative forces and management must be sure that it is actually needed before embarking on its introduction.

*Requirements for success*

Because change does release negative as well as positive forces within the college it can cause much stress and anxiety among staff, and can challenge the established organisational politics and power groupings. To stand any chance of success those introducing the change should set out to ensure that the following conditions are satisfied:

- Ownership: staff must feel a sense of ownership of the change being introduced from outside.
- Support: staff must feel and see that they are being supported in their efforts by senior managers.
- Values: the change must have a close match to the values of the staff involved in its implementation.
- Confidence/trust: staff must be sure that they have the confidence and trust of their colleagues and management as they go about introducing the change.
- Security: staff must be assured that the proposed change will not affect their job security.

## Identifying what needs changing

Before starting on the introduction of any change it is necessary to be clear abut what actually needs changing. The major problem, however, is that because of the social nature of colleges as organisations a simple curriculum change can often have a major impact on relationships within the organisation. Therefore, any form of analysis is difficult and can only be undertaken within a framework which combines a variety of elements all of which interact and inter-relate with each other as the change takes place.

In order to identify what needs to be changed a set of simple questions can be used as the framework for analysis. For example will the proposed change involve one or more of the following:

- Will it affect the nature of the current programme of services offered by the college?

  ♦ Changes in the structure or content of the curriculum or the addition of new ways for individuals to achieve accreditation are major forces in educational change.

- Will it require changes in behaviour?

  ♦ Changes in the ways in which staff are required to behave are often major elements required to support change.

- Will it require role or organisational change?

  ♦ Proposed changes often require changes in the roles performed by staff or in the ways in which these roles are arranged within the college's organisation.

- Will it bring about changes in the established social system of the college?

  ♦ This may be caused by the redistribution of power and influence due to changes in role or organisational configuration.

- Will the college's systems need adjusting to support the proposed change?

  ♦ Alterations in any of the financial or management information systems may be required to support the change. Systems 'lag' is always a problem associated with change because by their very nature they are designed to support the existing system and not the proposed changes.

It is important to put this analysis into the inter-related organisational framework described earlier.

*Types of change*

In addition to identifying what needs to be changed it is also necessary to be clear about the nature of the required change, and its potential impact on the existing situation. This form of analysis can be done through a check list which includes an impact assess- ment alongside each type of change, as follows:

| Type of change | Impact assessment | | | |
|---|---|---|---|---|
| | Low | | High | |
| Straight alteration to existing practices, modes of operation, staffing or organisation structure | A | B | C | D |
| Straight replacement of something already in existence | A | B | C | D |
| Extra addition to current system or practices | A | B | C | D |
| Removal of item(s) from established systems or practices | A | B | C | D |
| Restructuring of the existing systems or practices | A | B | C | D |

*The amount of change required*

Following on from the identification of what needs changing and the type of change required it is necessary to establish the amount of change required. This is particularly important from the point of view of understanding the amount of energy which is going to be required to bring the change about.

As with the earlier analysis the elements involved are not isolated and they will interact with one another and add to the complexity involved in bringing about the change.

The framework will need to be specific to the nature of the proposed change. However, the following will serve to illustrate the method:

- Changes in objectives: any major change of objectives will require energy to be expended to explain the reasons for change and gain commitment towards the new objectives. Extra monitoring and control may also be needed during the early stages of embedding and working towards new objectives.
- Changes in volume: increases or decreases in the amount of activity involved may require extra supervision or supportive help during the initial stages.
- Skills/knowledge changes: the amount of new skills/knowledge required from staff will need to be underpinned through effective staff training and development.
- Value changes: asking for changes in values is extremely difficult and can take a considerable amount of time and effort.

# Chapter 12

# Managing change: change models

There are many models which can be used to provide a framework for implementing change in colleges. The three most widely used approaches are:

1 Individual-orientated models: based on the role of the individual in bringing about change. These models usually begin with awareness raising and progress through to implementation.
2 Systems models: based on the view of change as an orderly process which can be systematically worked through during its implementation.
3 Management models: based on change being a managed process which can be brought about by careful preparation, planning and implementation.

All three approaches have been extensively applied to the management of change in further education. However, because they offer two contrasting perspectives of how educational change can be brought about the individual and management initiated models have been chosen for a more detailed analysis of their usefulness.

• The individual model because it demonstrates how change is brought about through the actions of individuals.
• The management model because it illustrates the growing importance of managed change in colleges.

The models operate at the two ends of the continuum of educational change, and both will continue to be important in the future. However, particular importance will be paid to the processes of managed change, on the grounds that as we advance into the future it is going to become more important for college managers to implement large-scale change.

The kind of college described in this book will require sensitive management of change as new services are introduced and traditional values are challenged. Openness and flexibility require new systems and new approaches, both of which will require high change agent skills if they are to be successfully introduced.

## AN INDIVIDUAL MODEL OF CHANGE

As in the past, individuals acting in the capacity of change agents will continue to play an important role in bringing about changes in colleges. There are many models which focus on the role of individuals, but perhaps the best one for illustrating this role in education is the 'social interaction model'.

In this model the unit of analysis is the individual member of staff, its focus being the individual's perception of, and response to, information on the need to change. The model is based on the assumption that the most effective means of disseminating information concerned with change is through personal contact, so the key to adoption will be the social interaction between members of the adopting group. The stages in the model include:

- Awareness: the initial stage when members of staff become aware of the nature of the proposed change. Lacking complete information, they may be motivated to search for more. Being aware of the need for change, they link it to a method of successfully bringing it about. They are therefore motivated towards taking action.
- Interest: building on this motivation, the individual members of staff begin to seek out additional information, but they have not yet fully formed a judgement on the usefulness of the change to their own situation. During this stage personal commitment towards the change either increases or declines.
- Evaluation: when sufficient information has been collected it is tested and mentally evaluated to match the outcome of the change to its anticipated situation. It is during this stage that the decision to put the change on trial is made.
- Trial: this is the 'real time' trial of the change within the working situation, when the change is implemented on a small scale to test out its effectiveness. This trial stage is critical in finalising the adoption or rejection of the proposed change.
- Adoption: following the trial the decision to move towards full implementation is made. Once the implementation stage

begins the change becomes progressively adopted by the whole college.

The potential adopter will increasingly search for additional information as progress through the various stages of the model is made. This collection of information will cover the whole spectrum of personal contacts through to printed matter and other forms of media presentation.

## A MANAGEMENT INITIATED MODEL OF CHANGE

Bearing in mind that the social interaction model is based on the role of individual members of staff in bringing about change, the alternative focus comes from change brought about by college management. This can be described as organisationally planned change, and is based on:

1 Being able to demonstrate clearly the need to implement the proposed change. This must be based on a clear analysis and understanding of the reasons, so that its advantages can be clearly shown to all those affected.
2 Developing as much involvement as possible in the change process and building up understanding and commitment. Ask the staff directly affected for their views on options to the proposed change.
3 Establishing a project manager and project team with responsibility for implementing the proposed changes. The project team should be cross-college in nature and drawn from different levels in the college's organisation.
4 Alternatively, appointing an external change agent to work with and advise the implementation team.
5 Giving the change a high profile, through an effective communication strategy including newsletters, logos and demonstration of its impact on the organisation.
6 Backing up the proposed changes with specially developed training and development activities which directly support those involved in implementing and embedding the proposed changes.
7 Celebrating the success of the change by rewarding and acknowledging the efforts of those associated with bringing it about.

**Implementation**

The implementation of management imposed change needs to be carefully thought through and implemented. The model described here sounds simplistic but it does help to bring about change in a way which reduces staff resistance and builds up support.

The basic model has five parts:

- Preparation: establishing the parameters of the proposed change and assessing its impact on the college.
- Planning: setting out the activities involved, the sequence of implementation and the resources and training needed to ensure success. This stage also involves appointing a project manager and establishing a multi-disciplined team with the range of skills needed for the successful implementation of the proposed change.
- Implementation and monitoring effectiveness: beginning the programme and managing the implementation strategy, including resource usage and staff training and development.
- Managing resistance: responding to any resistance and overcoming it through communication and demonstration of the advantages of the proposed change.
- Celebrating: acknowledging the success of the change and recognising and rewarding those responsible for its implementation.

Each of the stages will now be expanded and dealt with in more detail.

*Preparation*

Before even beginning to plan for the implementation of a particular change a number of factors should be taken into account. These include:

- Assessing the organisational readiness of the college to accept the proposed change:
    - ◆ Is the college ready to accept the impact of the proposed change? Does it have the energy and resources to implement it? What psychological damage will be done if the change is unsuccessful?

- What lessons were learnt from the last changes?

  ◆ Does the college have good experiences of dealing with change? What happened last time? Which parts of the college's organisation responded positively and which parts resisted change? Does the college have any experience of implementing the kind of change being proposed on this occasion?

- How critical is the change?

  ◆ Colleges need all the stability they can find. It is therefore important that change should not be undertaken unless it positively contributes to the college's effectiveness and future viability.

- Can the change be easily described?

  ◆ The change must be easy to describe and its advantages clearly demonstrated if it is to be communicated effectively to staff.

- Preparing the staff:

  ◆ Staff need preparation time to assess the impact of the proposed change on their methods of working and their role within the college's organisational and cultural structures.

It is only when these factors have been assessed and the college has confidence that the proposed change is needed that the planning stage should be embarked upon.


*Planning*

Once the decision to implement change has been taken the planning of its implementation can begin. This will involve the following steps:

- Identifying the critical success factors:

  ◆ The first stage of planning is that of identifying factors which are critical to the success of the proposed change.

- Identifying activities required for successful change:

  ◆ Arrange them into an action plan by listing them in the order of carrying them out. Estimate the time required to carry out each activity and the name of the individual responsible for carrying it out.

- Interference:
  - ◆ Allow for the impact of the change on the existing arrangement and whether it will interfere with the smooth running of the day-to-day operation. Where necessary, reduce the interference factor by arranging a temporary policy change to allow work to continue as flexibly as possible.
- Involvement:
  - ◆ Involve as many staff as possible in the planning stage.
- Management:
  - ◆ Appoint a project manager and project team to implement the action plans and take the necessary corrective action. The person appointed must have sufficient authority to ensure that the project stays on course.
- Communications:
  - ◆ Keep two-way communications as open as possible. Ensure that all staff receive information fast and use a variety of methods of communication, such as newsheets, hot lines, electronic mail boxes, video tapes, meetings, posters and training sessions.

*Implementation and monitoring*

The implementation and monitoring stage is crucial to introducing the change successfully and embedding it into the college's methods of working. The steps involved include:

- Monitoring and control:
  - ◆ Arrange for regular monitoring and control meetings which receive feedback on progress. These meetings will also control progress and draw up contingency plans where necessary to ensure eventual success.
- Observation:
  - ◆ Allow time to stand back and view the progress of implementation. Look for any additional opportunities created from the introduction of the change.

- Communication:
  - ◆ As with the preparation and planning stages, keep communications as open as possible, look for opportunities to collaborate and co-ordinate with other activities.
- Implementation:
  - ◆ Begin implementation in a step-by-step, planned way, building up staff confidence in the changed way of working.
- Training:
  - ◆ Link in training sessions to support the change and build up confidence in its successful outcome.
- Involvement:
  - ◆ Encourage staff involvement, self-management and problem solving within the objectives of the project. Encourage staff to think and act creatively.
- Resistance:
  - ◆ Allow for resistance, be ready to help staff overcome their problems and if necessary temporarily withdraw from the impact of the proposed change on their methods of working.
- Managing resistance:
  - ◆ Because of the importance of being able to identify and manage potential resistance the subject will be dealt with in detail in a section of its own (see Chapter 13).
- Celebrating:
  - ◆ Given the hard work involved in implementing change, it is important that its success is acknowledged publicly. This acknowledgement also encourages others to face up to the challenge of change and creates an organisational environment where it is seen to be acceptable to take the risks associated with change.

    Those responsible for the change should also be rewarded and their achievement acknowledged. Monetary reward is not always appropriate and time to implement the change effectively is perhaps the most important reward.

# Chapter 13

# Managing the resistance to change

Colleges are often criticised for their conservative approach towards change, along with their general resistance towards it. But in times of uncertainty, resistance can be a positive force as it sharpens the need for a clear demonstration of the improvements which may result from change. It is important to distinguish between resistance on the grounds that the proposed change:

1 is the wrong solution for an acknowledged problem; or
2 is irrelevant because there is no corresponding problem.

In both cases resistance encompasses any kind of activity which serves to maintain the status quo in the face of pressure to change it.

## LEVELS OF RESISTANCE

Resistance to change in colleges can be assessed at three levels:

1 individuals and their personal response to the change as it affects them directly;
2 groups of staff as they interact together within the organisation. They could be formal groups required by the organisation to work together or informal groups which are formed through psychological needs;
3 the whole organisation, due to lack of clarity or changes in the functional or power relationships.

Each of these levels will now be considered in more detail.

### Resistance at the individual level

Resistance at the individual level can originate from a number of sources, such as:

- lack of clarity about the nature of the change, which can be a major obstacle particularly when it results in:
  - ◆ resistance from individuals because they are unclear of the behaviour expected of them
  - ◆ inadequate planning, because communicating the requirements of change is difficult due to lack of clarity about its exact nature
  - ◆ incomplete information, which can lead to the abandonment of change
  - ◆ negative outcomes building up barriers to the future introduction of change.
- selective perception and retention, which can be one of the most important psychological barriers against change. It may result in the individual not being able to see that the existing situation is inadequate, and in those directly concerned not being able to recognise the problem or see any solution to it.
- when the initiator and the group both recognise the problem but are unable to share a common perception of its nature and course, resulting in a different perception of how the remedy should be applied.
- staff insecurity, which can be important, particularly when it manifests itself in uncertainty and anxiety about the ability to perform. Management expectations and the heavy use of evaluation systems may also result in insecurity and, through it, resistance to change.
- conformity and commitment to past practices, which can be a major force of resistance to new situations.
- personality factors, which can cause individual barriers to change. These can include:
  - ◆ low emphatic ability
  - ◆ high dogmatism
  - ◆ inability to deal with abstraction
  - ◆ low motivation.
- a change advocate who is unable to describe adequately the requirements of the change.

### Resistance at the level of groups of staff

The social dimension within college organisation becomes particularly important when considering the introduction of a proposed change. Within the organisational context many of the barriers are linked into the dynamics of group behaviour, the important ones being:

- Group solidarity, which becomes a form of resistance when the change threatens the cohesiveness of the group.
- Group culture, which is important particularly when the change agent is seen to come from a different culture. The group may then view their own culture as superior and resist the imposition of another.

  Even when staff have been involved in formulating the change they may be reluctant to adopt it if they were not adequately involved in defining the problem to which the change is addressed.

  Finally, the different cultural perspectives held by the two parties may result in different expectations of what the change will achieve.

- Conformity to norms, which provide stability and the behaviourial guidelines for operating within the group, and are therefore essential to the effective functioning of the group as a social system. Any proposed change which is incompatible with these norms will be resisted.

  The critical question is: 'Why do members of the group participate in the maintenance of the norm?' The answer to this may enable the change to be modified to meet the norm expectations of the group.

- Group insight, or lack of it, which may reach the point where the group is unaware of its own interpersonal processes. Coupled to the lack of a frame of reference against which they can judge their own performance, the group will not be able to perceive the need to improve. The building of a frame of reference, along with feedback loops on performance, may therefore be critical in removing barriers to change.

- Conflict and frustration, which arises when change is proposed by a group which is already in conflict with those who are expected to implement the proposed change. The second group may then automatically reject the idea because it has originated from the group with which they are in conflict.

The positive side of conflict is its use as a force for bringing about change. Conflict often causes those involved in it to be thoughtful when expressing their respective views, with the result that each has a more carefully constructed position towards change. This is particularly true when those arguing from one position are challenged by their opponents. Where their position is likely to damage the effectiveness of the college, they are more likely to take this into account and to develop remedial contingency plans for the consequences of their actions.

### Resistance at the organisational level

Change is often required at the level of the college's organisation, particularly when new roles and responsibilities are being introduced, and certain structural characteristics of organisations may either facilitate or resist change. Resistance may exist at this level because:

- Established and highly formalised structures often want to stick with their existing ways of doing things.
- Fresh-start organisations may offer resistance to change, particularly if the pressures follow quickly after start-up problems have been overcome.
- Complex organisations which have to perform a range of different tasks are often more open to change than less complex rigid structures.
- Organisations with well established power structures often find it difficult to implement any form of change which appears to reduce the established power.
- Decentralised organisations often find it easier to implement change, providing there are not too many parts in the organisation.
- Organisations with a large number of gatekeepers, who can exercise control and manipulate the flow of information, are often very difficult to change.
- The existence of unclear role definition, or authority structures, can result in resistance due to confusion and uncertainty.
- Poor communications within the college can provide another source of resistance. Although effective upwards communication is an important element in management control, the fact that staff often experience their problems in self-contained classrooms provides them with little opportunity to convey to management problems which require attention.

- Low involvement in decision-making, particularly when it is limited to a narrow range of staff such as heads of department, often provides little opportunity for innovation due to the lack of staff freedom to introduce new ideas.
- Poor management and weak leadership leading to low risk-taking often acts as a brake on the need for the organisation to face up to the need for change.
- Organisations have a tendency to be homeostatic, that is, to remain unchanged. There are many factors which may cause homeostasis, the main ones being reluctance to admit weaknesses, the awkwardness and fear of failure associated with doing something new, bad experiences with past change efforts, and concern about the possible loss of present satisfaction.

# Index

'A' levels 13
academic characteristics 79
academic education 64; *see also*
    vocational education
academic qualifications 13; *see
    also* vocational qualifications
access 1, 20, 27, 33, 52, 54, 69;
    barriers to 17, 70, 87–8;
    progression of 33
access and guidance services 90;
    accreditation of prior learning
    90; diagnostic testing 90;
    induction programmes to
    support literacy, numeracy
    and communication skills 90;
    learning styles assessment 90;
    portfolio building and
    presentation 90; support into
    learning 90
accessibility and openness 52,
    57, 67, 74
accountability 5
accreditation 7–8, 16, 18–19, 27,
    29, 31, 38, 45, 49, 54, 88, 91, 103
accreditation of employers'
    training, the 54
accreditation of non-traditional
    learning, the 90
accreditation of prior learning
    (APL), the 1–8, 10, 25, 27–8,
    32–4, 37–44, 52, 71, 75, 80, 82,
    90, 93, 97, 100, 102; *see also* the
    recognition of prior learning
accreditation of work-based

learning, the 14–15, 25, 45–6,
    48; *see also* work-based
    learning
accreditation options 8
accreditation services 37–48, 71,
    85
accreditation, the introduction
    of 7
achievement-based
    qualifications 53
achievement-focused funding 13
achievement opportunities
    networks 55
achievement recognition 33, 35,
    37
action planning/scheduling 35
activity/preparation 6; potential
    population for accreditation 6
actual demand 68
actual students 84, 87
administrative structures 4
administrative systems 5;
    bureaucracy 5; management
    systems 5; paperwork 5
admission stage, the 79–80
admissions 83
advanced diplomas 13
advice and guidance 80
advice stage, the 79–80
age 64
aggregate demand 72
aggregate funds 76–7
alternative fee-waiving
    strategies 70; *see also* the

Made in the USA
Lexington, KY
11 April 2014